Getting Started in
Handmade Rugs

Books in the *Getting Started* series

Getting Started in
Handmade Rugs

KATHRYN ANDREWS MARINOFF

Revision of *Handmade Rugs*

The Bruce Publishing Company / New York
Collier-Macmillan Limited / London

Library of Congress Catalog Card Number: 77–160380

THE BRUCE PUBLISHING COMPANY
866 THIRD AVENUE, NEW YORK, NEW YORK 10022

COLLIER-MACMILLAN CANADA, LTD., TORONTO, ONTARIO

Made in the United States of America

ACKNOWLEDGMENTS

The many people who have crossed my path over the years have each contributed something to this book. To all of them and especially to those named below I express my gratitude:

Constance B. Schrader and Susan C. Shipman of the Bruce Publishing Company for their encouragement and helpfulness in this revision of my earlier book;

Marilyn Léon of Michigan for the Flossa rug which she designed and wove, and which was displayed in the New Mexico International Folk Art Museum, Santa Fe;

Rebecca James for her beautiful example of the Colcha stitch, also from the New Mexico International Folk Art Museum, Santa Fe;

George Downing, artist and teacher, for his carefully drawn braided-rug illustrations;

Mrs. Louise Pote for the black-and-white photos of the primitive loom, braided rugs, stair treads, rug woven on the loom, and the Carriage Wheel Whirl;

Philippine Fanning for her drawings;

Frieda Z. Tuinsma for her interest and cooperation in supplying the colorful Rya rug, one of her many prizewinning pieces;

Lloyd Rule and James B. De Korne for their colored photos, and for their interest and efforts in photographing the best possible examples;

Winifred Hare of Columbus, Ohio, who not only hooked the rug in Plate 3, but also obtained the picture;

Vivian Bardwell for the rectangular braided rug, type A;

Catherine Downing for the shirred rug in Plate 7;

Frances Sargent for lending the blue-and-white open cross-stitched rug;

Rebecca Moyer for the carpet-remnant rug which she designed and assembled;

The New Mexico International Folk Art Museum, Santa Fe, and Leise and Wally Sargent for their cooperation in arranging for the photography.

Last and certainly not least I wish to express my heartfelt appreciation to my family, whose encouragement and help were constant; and to my students who, over the years, have inspired me to learn more in order to give more.

CONTENTS

To my mother,
Myrtle Andrews Gere

INTRODUCTION

If you have never made a rug before, why not try your hand at it? The rug can be knotted, hooked, woven, or braided. The designs of today's floor coverings allow unlimited possibilities for creative activity, self-expression, and artistry.

Rugmaking is a popular as well as a traditional hobby, which fosters congeniality and the exchange of new and old ideas. For many it offers a new way of life. Because it includes a wide variety of styles and methods ranging from the traditional to the contemporary, rugmaking spans all age groups and areas of taste.

Making something of your own is always a rewarding experience. Colors, materials, and ideas are everywhere. It's simple to make rugs of any style, color, and texture which will add beauty and warmth to your surroundings. Why not begin today? There's always time for the things you want to do, and creating something for one's home is very satisfying.

Hopefully this book will inspire you to start a small area or accent rug of your own. Design and create it yourself or copy your patterns. Using other people's drawings, however, will soon prove unsatisfactory, for you will want to express yourself by individual, original, and daring uses of color and arrangements of materials. Make your rug "way out" if you choose. It's yours. Of all the many techniques explained in *Handmade Rugs*, surely you will find the method that suits your talents and your taste.

1

KNOTTED RUGS

THE RYA RUG

The Rya rug, one of the simplest and quickest you can make, is a Swedish knotted rug (Plate 1). Its surface has a shaggy cut pile which is the result of knotting Rya wool yarn. If you have not tried making a rug using the Rya knot technique, you've missed something. An established craftsman will progress rapidly and the beginner will soon catch up and enjoy the same feeling of accomplishment.

Design

The color and design of a Rya rug will please even the most contemporary taste. Since it is not suitable for a very detailed design, this knotted rug is a project which appeals to every beginner. Design ideas are everywhere. Your inspiration may come from a sunset, a raging river, snow-capped mountains, or colorful flowers and trees. Most of all, the design should please you, the creator. Keep in mind that large areas of color are more effective than small patches.

The Rya rug can be made in squares 16 inches or larger, which are later sewed together. These small sections are easy to carry with you wherever you go. Families who move frequently find the Rya rug convenient because its size can be altered according to need.

Materials

1. The foundation for the Rya rug is an imported double-mesh canvas made of 49 percent cotton and 51 percent hemp. Because it is sturdy and smooth, this canvas is a pleasure to work with. A more expensive backing is a Danish canvas — 30 percent wool, 36 percent linen, and 34 percent cut rayon. Cut whichever product you choose 1 inch larger than the size of the finished rug.

   If the conventional foundation is not available, a single canvas can be substituted. In this case two threads will replace the heavier double-canvas bar on the imported canvas. You may have to resort to a good grade of burlap. If so, draw two threads across the rug to form the knotting channel. Leave a row of five threads undrawn between each channel. Machine-stitch a double hem ¼ inch wide all around the edge. The finished rug should be faced with a piece of burlap for added strength.

2. Rya yarn is available in different weights and colors. You can combine several in one needle to give a variegated effect. The amount of yarn necessary varies according to the size of the rug, its design, and color arrangement.

3. You will need several large, blunt canvas or tapestry needles, either curved or straight. Have several threaded ahead of time so that they will be ready when you want to change colors.

4. A gauge with which to measure the pile will be needed. A 12-inch ruler can be used.

5. A grease pencil.

   Commercial rugmaking kits can be purchased in most needlework departments in stores. These include needles, yarn, gauge, canvas, and design. For many, this is an easy way to gather materials. You can follow the pattern suggested in the kit or use your own design.

   Needlework catalogues list suppliers of rugmaking materials. If you do not live where materials are for sale, these lists can be extremely useful in helping you obtain them.

Procedure

1. Stitch a narrow hem around the edge of the canvas foundation if it doesn't already have a woven border.

2. With a grease pencil, draw your design on the canvas. Number each section and key these numbers to a color chart, or thread a short piece of yarn through the canvas for quick color identification.

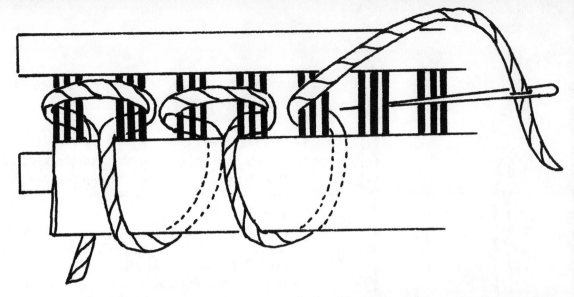

FIGURE 1   Making a Ghiordes knot. Gauge
inserted.

3. Cut the skeins of yarn into lengths of not more than 36 inches.

4. Thread several canvas needles.

5. Begin to work at the lower left-hand corner of the rug. Place the needle with the rug yarn into the center of the first square of threads (Figure 1). Pull the needle under the three left threads.

6. Pull the yarn through to the left, leaving an inch-long tail hanging down.

7. Swing the threaded needle back to the right. Come over and under the three right threads, ending in the center where you first entered.

8. Place the gauge over the right-hand thread. Bring the needle over the top, holding the gauge steady (this measures the length of the loop).

9. Pull the yarn down. This forms the knot called the Turkey, or Ghiordes (pronounced *Yor-deez*) knot. Do not make it too tight.

10. Put the needle into the center of the next square of threads and proceed as in Steps 5-9.

11. Continue across the canvas from left to right, changing yarn colors when designated by the pattern. Push the gauge to the right as you continue knotting.

12. When a row is finished, cut the yarn along the edge of the gauge for an even pile. If you want a more shaggy, uneven pile, pull out the gauge and clip one loop at a time.

13. Start sewing the second row at the lower left-hand side above the first row and continue working to the right tying knots. You may acquire sufficient rhythm and accuracy to be able to work without the gauge; many

KNOTTED RUGS

needleworkers do. As your rug grows, roll it up to keep it out of your way.

THE FLOSSA RUG

The Flossa rug (Plate 2) is similar to the Rya rug, for both are made with the Ghiordes knot. The difference between the two is in the pile, which stands up straighter on the Flossa rug. This is because the rod or gauge, which is 3/8 to 3/4 inches wide, produces a shorter pile. In the Rya rug the pile is longer. In addition, the Flossa rug has two tabby, or plain, weaves between each row of knots that give these areas a flat surface. (Tabby, the simplest and one of the most frequently used weaves, is made by taking the weft under and over the warp.) If a longer pile is desired, use a wider gauge and more rows of tabby in between. The rug shown in Plate 2 has varying pile lengths.

THE LATCH-NEEDLE RUG

Unlike the Rya rug which is made with a canvas needle, this knotted rug is made with a latch needle or, as it is sometimes called, a latch hook (Figure 2). This is a mechanical needle used by many craftsmen, and because it is a time-saving device, it has become very popular. The latch at the top of the needle opens and closes. When the latch is closed, it is in contact with the point of the hook, or needle. When it is open, it lies flat against the shank, or stalk — the metal part of the needle between the wooden handle and the hook — so that there are no protruding parts to catch onto the canvas.

Like the Rya rug, this latch-needle rug has a shaggy pile, the length of which is determined by the length of the yarn. It is perfect for the bedroom, living room, and even the bath. In a long strip it adds color and interest to a hallway. Made in squares or strips which are sewed together, it becomes a large rug or carpeting.

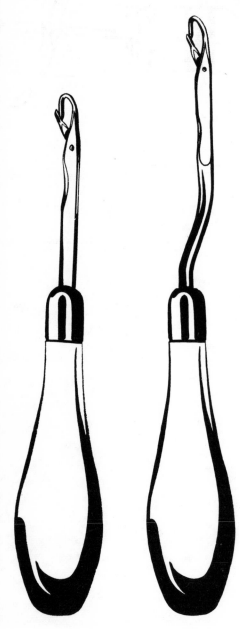

FIGURE 2 Latch needles.

Design

The design for this knotted rug can be very loose and free of detail. Sources of inspiration for a modern abstract design are all around you — reflections in a pool, cloud configurations, or a field of flowers. Your friends may not recognize where your pattern originated from or even what it is, but that is of little consequence since you've had a wonderful time creating it.

Materials

1. Use a single canvas backing, allowing an inch all around for a hem.
2. Cut pieces of wool, orlon, or rayon-and-cotton-blended rug yarn. To cut the yarn, wrap it carefully around a cardboard and cut along one edge. It is a good idea to make sample loops, using 3, 4, and 5 inch lengths of yarn to determine the height you prefer.
3. A latch needle (formerly called the Dritz latch).
4. A frame (optional, since this rug can be made either on a frame or on your lap).

Procedure

1. Block off the design and designate the color to be used on the right side of the canvas. This is the side on which you will be tying the knots.
2. Hem the canvas, turning under the 1-inch edge allowed.
3. Begin working in the lower left-hand corner of the rug. Open the latch of the needle by pressing it back flat against the stalk (Figure 3). Slip the latch needle through the square of canvas, and from this position put it into the square of canvas above. Lay the cut piece of yarn under the shank of the needle and pull the two ends of the yarn together at the top.
4. From the right side, still holding the yarn ends together, bring them around in back of the needle, and forward under the hook.
5. Close the latch with your left hand. Guide the hook as you pull the handle down with your right hand. The hook slides through the square, then through the loop of yarn. Presto, your first knot is tied. How simple! As you work, develop a rhythm. Like magic, knots begin to cover the canvas.
6. Take another piece of yarn. Tie the next knot in the square to the right. When row one is finished, move to the row above and begin working from left to right. You will be surprised at how fast your supply of cut yarn disappears. You'll need to cut more. Already a colorful area has been knotted. You're on your way.

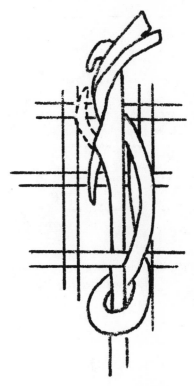

FIGURE 3 Use of the latch needle.

THE TUFTED RUG

This is a simple and pleasing little rug which is inexpensive, decorative, and useful. It fits in any place.

FIGURE 4 Tying tufts to the foundation for the tufted rug.

Design

Create a very simple design or use as much detail as you wish. If you begin by making a plain rug, you may wish to make your next project more colorful. Autumn leaves might suggest a design of fall colors — yellows, oranges, and browns. The ocean might inspire a rug of green, blue, and white. Simply look around you!

Materials

1. Use a burlap sack, monk's cloth, or any heavy, firm material for the foundation.
2. Yarn or cotton thread.
3. A canvas needle.
4. A crayon.
5. Cardboard.
6. Scissors.

Procedure

1. With a colored crayon, mark dots 1/2 inch apart on the foundation. Place the dots in either straight or staggered lines (Figure 4).
2. Wrap the yarn or cotton thread around a 1-inch board or heavy card about twenty times, depending on the thickness of your material. Fluffy yarn requires less winding.
3. When the material is wrapped, carefully slip it off the board; then with a 4-inch piece of yarn, tie a knot at one end of the tuft to hold it together. The tails of the yarn left hanging will be used to anchor the tuft to the foundation.
4. Thread one tail and pull it through one of the dots to the back of the foundation. Bring it back up to the top. Unthread the needle and duplicate this step with the other tail.
5. Now both ends are on top. Tie them together in a firm knot and snip off any surplus. The tuft is now secured to the foundation.
6. After all the tufts have been attached to the rug's surface (Figure 4), clip each one open with a pair of sharp scissors, thereby forming the pile of your rug.
7. To finish the edges, attach facing to the back with an additional piece of material. If the border is large enough, use it for facing. Cut out some of the surplus material on the corner and form a neat, flat, mitered corner.

2

HOOKED RUGS

The hooked rug (Plate 3) is made by pushing wool yarn or strips of woolen cloth back and forth through a canvas or burlap foundation. How the material is worked and how the rug is designed are a matter of choice, since techniques are changing so rapidly.

For those who like the traditional, the ideals are still detailed design and fine workmanship. Fine woolen yarns and strips, and the Susan Bates steel needle, are the equipment of the traditional craftsman. He wants none of the mechanical implements that measure the loop and save time. In a sense these craftsmen help to keep the art of rug hooking alive by their insistence on traditional tools, methods, and designs.

The new craftsman, however, is very contemporary in spirit. He is happy to use such mechanical tools as the Susan Burr shuttle needle, the Columbia Minerva hook, or the walking hook. These tools ensure accuracy by regulating the stitches and the height of the pile, and they are noticeably faster than the hand hook.

Design
Design concepts are also viewed in different ways by the traditional and the contemporary craftsmen.

For the contemporary, design is perhaps the first consideration. He often departs from the traditional techniques to suit his own needs. Since he does not aspire to making a fine painting, he has no need for intricate stitches or detailed shading. Instead he prefers geometric designs which emphasize line and texture. This modern craftsman is not inhibited or controlled by any given pattern; he is free to express his creativity and versatility in many ways. His imagination is stimulated by psychedelic wallpapers, modern paintings, and even museum collages.

Color is of primary importance to the contemporary. He is daring in his use of vivid reds, blues, oranges, and yellows. He might tie-dye the burlap backing and then hook the bold, colorful design that results. Texture is another element that is important to his design. The pile may be cut at irregular levels; some loops are clipped and some are not. Colorful yarns of varying weights produce an interesting texture as does the use of foreign materials such as sisal, plastic fiber, fur, grasses, and feathers. The contemporary might make a round rug, using small wedge effects to display these materials. When his project is completed, the contemporary feels rewarded. The products are unique because they are his own.

To those who prefer the traditional hooked rug, these methods may seem undisciplined and haphazard. This is the reaction of a craftsman with an established background. He has seen beautifully detailed and shaded hooked rugs in museums. He has studied illustrations of rugs which resemble fine oil paintings and are realistic rather than abstract. His inspiration comes from delicate patterns on antique china, flower arrangements in gardens and shops, and beautiful old mellow-colored quilts. Even the prints of Currier and Ives are inspiration for those who dream of another era.

There are, therefore, two very different areas of design available to the craftsman. The choice depends solely on preference. However, certain basic points have to be considered whether you plan to buy, stencil, trace, copy, or create your own design. As a yardstick for selecting the right design, regardless of the type of home you have, ask yourself these basic questions:

Does your design have balance? Is it in scale with the rug for which it is intended?

Does your design have rhythm? Do all parts agree in shape and scale? Do its lines draw your eyes around the room?

Does the design suit the room's décor? Is the room formal, informal, simple, elaborate? Is it contemporary or period? Historical or regional?

Is your design too realistic for the place in which it will be used?

Is the design in proportion to the surface on which it will be used? To the room? To the contour of the area it is to cover?

Does the material suit the design? Does it suit the type of hooking you will be doing?

Is the distribution of color right for the design?

Are the curved and straight lines in correct proportion?

Is the design stylized or abstract?

Does the design interfere with the rug's function?

Finally, does the design please you? If it doesn't, you won't do your best work.

Materials

1. The filler, which consists of yarns of all shades, colors, and weights, will determine what your rug will look like. The contemporary will be "wilder" in his choice of colors, and his yarn will be heavier since he wants to project less detail. But color is important to both styles. The detail of traditional work calls for a finer yarn, and more colors and shades to produce a realistic effect.

   Some of our most cherished rugs are made of material rather than yarn. Woven material makes beautiful rugs when workmanship is of prime importance. Dyeing materials, collecting swatches of many different shades, and cutting fine strips can be less expensive than buying yarns. There are still firms which specialize in selling swatches of woolen material to many experts in rug hooking. If you wish to gather your own woolen material, however, the following directions for its preparation will be helpful.

   a. Be particular in the selection of your materials. Use only those which have fast colors (test by washing in water) and be sure all materials are clean. Use soft, pliable weaves such as jersey, flannel, cashmere, or challis, but eliminate gabardines or men's suiting. A good rule is to eliminate any fabric which might take a good crease in pressing.

      Old garments will be very useful if the worn portions are discarded. Hold the material up to the light in order to detect any tiny moth holes or thin areas. Select only the good sections of your used woolens so that your rug will be long-wearing. This is especially important if you plan to combine old and new materials.

b. To prepare used materials for hooking, air them and shake well. Rip out all seams. Remove buttons, pockets, linings, cuffs, collars. Test for color fastness. Wash and dry (this is very simple if an automatic washer is used). Dye, if desired. Tear into strips—this can be done by hand or with a commercial cutter (Figure 5) Making swatches gets to be a game. You can't seem to get enough shades of each color to satisfy you. The least variation in dyeing produces many more different shades.

2. The foundation can be a good grade of burlap or a two-ply monk's cloth, each of which makes a sturdy background. Smaller pieces can be hooked and then sewed together if you wish to make a larger rug later. If you are making a single rug that is not too large, allow sufficient foundation material for a 3-inch hem all around.

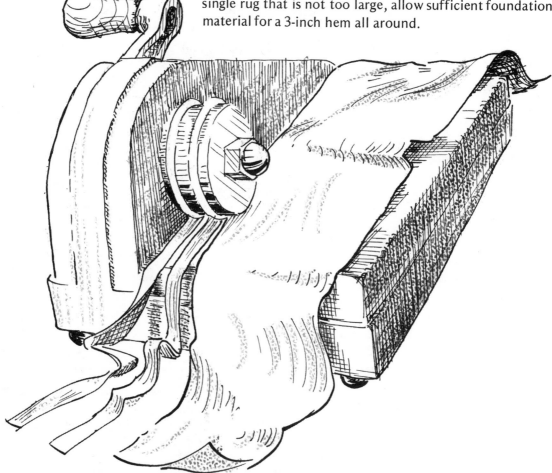

FIGURE 5   A commercial swatch-cutter.

3. Frames for hooking rugs can be made or purchased. New frames can be purchased at prices ranging from five to ten dollars or more. The least expensive type is easy to carry around and is very satisfactory. It resembles the homemade frame suggested below. The more expensive easel style (Figure 6) has an adjustable bar across the top and bottom which makes it easy to roll up a large rug.

Homemade frames (Figure 7) can be made easily. Begin by cutting two pieces of 1 x 2 inch lumber into 28-inch lengths and two pieces into 40-inch lengths. One inch in from the end of these pieces, cut slots 1/4 inch wide and 4 inches long. Put a bolt with a wing nut through each corner where the slots pass over each other (Figure 7). These make it possible for you to adjust the frame to your work.

A frame can also be made from a discarded card table

FIGURE 7   Homemade frame for hooking rugs.

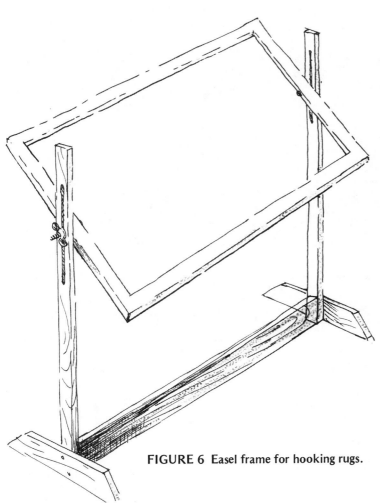

FIGURE 6 Easel frame for hooking rugs.

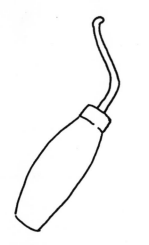

FIGURE 8 Susan Bates hand needle.

by removing the top but leaving the legs. This works very well if the rug is not too wide.

4. Needles. For the traditional rug the Susan Bates hand needle (Figure 8) or one like it is preferred. This is a hand needle with either a straight or curved shank which can be used with yarn or woolen strips. However, if you are familiar with the other styles described below and wish to use them, that is your choice. A fine crochet hook with a short wooden handle is sometimes substituted for this needle.

The mechanical type needles have proved to be especially popular with the contemporary rugmaker. The Susan Burr, a shuttle style hook which is worked with two hands (Figure 9), and the Columbia Minerva hook (Figure 10), known as the hollow handle needle, both produce very even and satisfactory work.

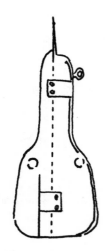

FIGURE 9 Susan Burr shuttle hook.

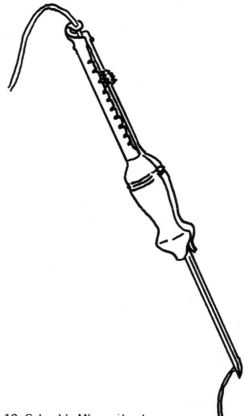

FIGURE 10 Columbia Minerva hook.

GETTING STARTED IN HANDMADE RUGS

Procedure

1. When working with the Susan Bates hand needle, the rug can be held on the lap. However, some beginners find that using a frame to hold the background taut makes hooking easier. In this case the burlap is anchored with thumbtacks or laced onto the frame. Outline the design first and then fill in this outline with stitches. Leave the background to be filled in last.

   When using this needle, work from the top, or on the right side of the pattern facing you. With the needle in the right hand, push it down through the backing to the underside (Figure 11). Hold the yarn or filler very taut on the underside with your left hand between your index finger and thumb. The hook picks up the yarn and brings it through to the top surface where it stays. This first stitch is a short tail, not a loop.

   Put the needle down again through the background picking up the wool. This time, bring it up to the top in the form of a loop (Figure 12). It is important to regulate the loops, keeping them about 3/8 inch high. Later these loops may be clipped, left as they are, or even bevelled. It is an excellent idea to practice hooking before you start on the rug you are making.

   If you are hooking with woolen strips instead of woolen yarn, cut the strips 1/8 inch wide on the straight grain. With very heavy rug wool, it may be necessary to skip two threads or more on the foundation between stitches to prevent crowding.

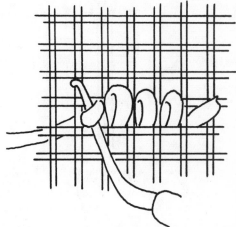

FIGURE 12 Making loops with the Susan Bates needle.

FIGURE 11 First steps in using the Susan Bates needle.

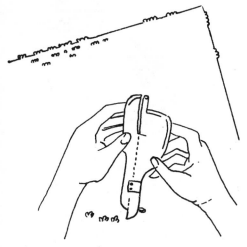

FIGURE 13 Using the Susan Burr shuttle hook.

2. When working with the Susan Burr shuttle hook, fasten the rug firmly to a frame. The wrong side of the rug should face up. Insert the needle from this side (Figure 13).

3. The Columbia Minerva hook is also worked with the rug wrong side up. Put the threaded needle into the foundation in a vertical position (Figure 14). It will go to a given point and stop, measuring the yarn for each stitch. The result is an even pile on the underside that becomes the right side when the rug is finished. Because there are several size fittings for this needle, there is a possible choice of yarn weights for different rugs. This also makes the use of woolen strips possible. Practice on another piece of burlap until you feel secure in your work. Develop a rhythm to speed up your hooking.

4. When your rug is hooked, turn the hem flat against the back and overcast it down. Mitered corners help to keep the rug smooth. For the most satisfactory results, press your hooked rug by placing it face down on a padded surface. Dampen an old bed sheet in warm water and press the rug with a medium hot iron. Allow the rug to dry completely.

5. When dry, turn the rug with its right side to the floor. Paint this surface with Saf-T-Back, a liquid substance which seals and prevents the rug from slipping on a slick floor. One quart covers 12 square feet. Let it dry.

6. To protect your beautiful rug from soil, spray the right side with Sta-Clean. This is a harmless silicone product which keeps "spills" from penetrating the pile and makes it possible to wipe off soil. Scotchgard, another fine product, also serves as a protective coating.

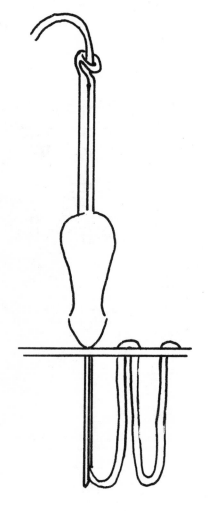

FIGURE 14 Using the Columbia Minerva hook.

GETTING STARTED IN HANDMADE RUGS

3

WEAVING

The art of weaving is an ancient craft. It is done on a loom which consists of a series of lengthwise threads called the warp into which is woven a crosswise series of threads called the weft, or filler. Even today the basic principles of weaving are the same as those employed by primitive man; only the machinery has changed. The technology of machines and the ingenuity of man have changed the art of weaving from a handcraft into a highly mechanized and efficient mass-production system.

Because the principles of weaving have remained the same (Figure 15 and Plate 4), basic looms are still successful tools which are fun to use. The simple looms include the backstrap, or waist, loom; the upright loom; and the carriage wheel whirl. The popsicle loom is a very simple, easy-to-make home loom.

THE BACKSTRAP, OR WAIST, LOOM

Throughout Central America men and women can be seen weaving beside their homes along the roadway. The backstrap loom that they use is primitive in style, but it is still found in many parts of the world. The loom in Plate 5, one of the oldest types, is Guatemalan. The branch across the top of the loom is

FIGURE 15 A Cherokee design woven on a modern loom.

Woven by Margaret Johnson

warped with strings which are wrapped onto another stick at the bottom. These supports are crude pieces of wood taken from a tree or willow and made slick by peeling them clean. The top piece has a rope tied at each end and the center of the rope is secured to a tree or post. The sticks across the top and the bottom form the loom and are slightly wider than the woven fabric will be. The stick closest to the body is fastened at each end to a wide band of net or cloth which goes around the weaver's hips just below the waist.

The shuttles are smooth sticks wrapped with the yarn which is to be woven into fabric. They are threaded through the warp opening, called the shed, which is formed by a shed stick. When the strands of wool have gone through, the shed is closed. The shed stick is then laid flat and forced against the weft several times to push the fibers together. This may be repeated several times before the weaver is satisfied. The weaver moves up closer to her work as the fabric is woven and she rolls it up from the bottom and ties the ends to hold it. This is not fast work and the strips are not very wide. However, when the finished strips are sewed together, they can make a room-sized rug. You can make this little loom yourself and use it just as it was used centuries ago.

THE POPSICLE LOOM

This improvised loom is a miniature of the waist loom. It is not large enough to make a rug, but since strips can be made almost any length you choose, they serve admirably as trim for a rug, when used with a woolen, or even a canvas, foundation. What these few sticks can do is unbelievable. Even if you are not a devoted weaver, working with the popsicle loom will help you to realize why people become so involved with this craft.

Materials
1. 25 popsicle sticks (or 12 can be used).
2. Yarn, flax, or twine.
3. Glue.

FIGURE 16 Sticks arranged for the popsicle loom (detail).

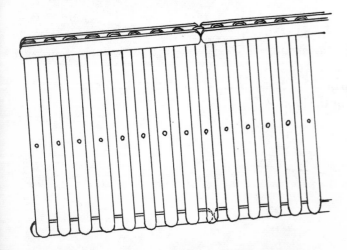

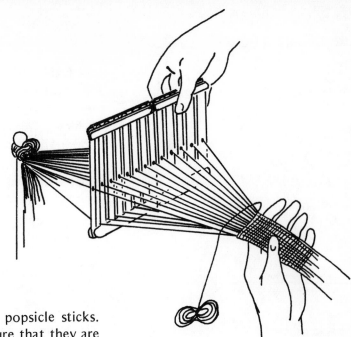

FIGURE 17 Using the popsicle loom.

Procedure

1. Drill holes in the center of 17 of the popsicle sticks. Arrange them as in Figure 16, making sure that they are evenly spaced.

2. Eight undrilled sticks will be needed—for the top of the loom and for the bottom. Between these, glue the ends of the drilled vertical sticks, as shown in Figure 16. One of the vertical sticks should be glued over the point where the two crosspieces touch.

3. When the glue is dry, "dress" the loom. Run a piece of yarn, flax, or twine through each center hole (Figure 17). These should all be of the same length, which is determined by the measurements of the finished work.

4. Now thread cords of the same length between each stick. If these threads are a different color from the first group, they will be easier to identify when you are weaving.

5. Pull and tie the threads together on the end farthest from you. Fasten them to a chair or hook. Hold the ends nearest you together. Tilt the popsicle-stick assembly which is the warp lifter, or heddle. This movement opens the shed, or the area through which the shuttle passes. Insert your index finger to serve as a shed stick. Weave the yarn that you selected for the weft through the opening.

6. Shift the heddle again or use a comb to tighten the weft threads against one another. Shift the heddle once more and carry the weft across again. After going back and forth a few times you will be surprised to see the pattern developing.

This little loom can be carried with you wherever you go. How fast your piece seems to grow now that you have really "caught on" to working with it!

THE UPRIGHT LOOM

The popsicle loom is a very simple device, useful only for producing small goods. If you don't have a commercial loom on which to make a complete rug, it can be done on an upright loom which you can make yourself.

Materials

1. A pair of discarded oak curtain stretchers which are available in salvage shops provides the material for the frame. Because they are hardwood, they hold the nails more securely and will not split. Other lumber can be substituted. I have seen old screen doors used when there was nothing else available.

2. Three-inch finishing nails, and bolts or clamps.

3. Heavy cord, warping twine, or strips of cloth selvage edge.

4. A shuttle is necessary to carry the weft over and under the warp. There are many types. It can be a 12-inch ruler with an eye to hold the filler (Figure 18) or you might make one out of a wider piece of wood with notches at the ends around which the weft can be wrapped.

5. Use a yardstick to make warp sticks. When tipped on edge, these sticks open the shed to allow the weft to pass through (Figure 18).

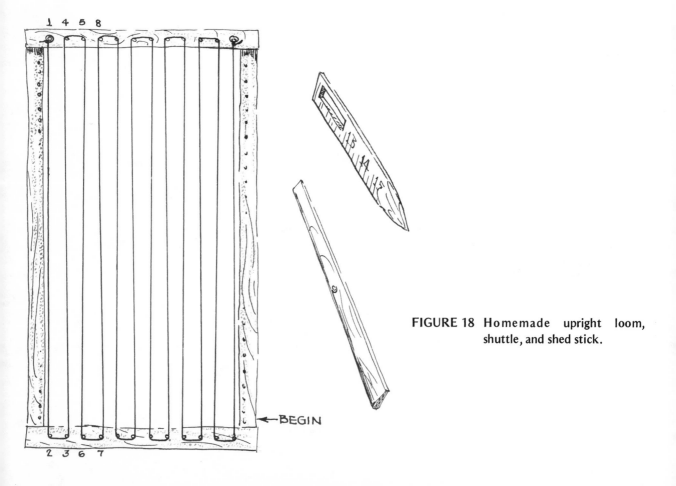

FIGURE 18 Homemade upright loom, shuttle, and shed stick.

6. Yarn, or strips of woolen or cotton cloth can be used for the filler. If material is used, strips should be cut 1½ inches wide and the edges should be turned so that they don't ravel.

Procedure

1. Use two full 72-inch lengths of the stretchers for the sides of the frame. Cut two more into 40-inch lengths to use as the top and the bottom. If the frame is light-weight, another 40-inch length piece should be cut and placed through the center on the underside as a support.

2. Bolt or clamp the corners together.

3. Insert finishing nails along the top, bottom, and side frame pieces 1 inch in from the edge and ½ inch apart. These nails will support the warp and the weft. You may have to drill holes to make it easier to insert the nails. Stagger the nails slightly to prevent splitting the wood.

4. Starting at the upper left-hand corner (Figure 18), tie the warp on with a slip knot. Guide the warp from the upper left-hand corner to the lower left-hand corner. Go around in back of nails numbers 2 and 3. Keep the warp very tight and return to the top. Go in back of nails 4 and 5. Continue doing this all the way across, until the loom is completely warped. Then fasten the end on the upper right-hand nail.

5. After the loom is completed, thread the shuttle and insert the warp, or shed, sticks, by weaving them under and over the warp. One goes under and over, the other goes over and under; both are put in flat. When "tipped on edge," the first stick opens the path for the shuttle carrying the weft to slip through.

6. Start to weave at the lower right-hand corner, running the shuttle in 6 or more inches above the nails. This leaves enough cord to make a short fringed or knotted edge.

7. When the left side is reached, lay one shed stick flat, and tip the other one on edge to open the way for the weft to weave to the right. Fold in the edges of the material as you weave. It will be necessary to beat the weft tightly against itself as you progress. With this loom a heavy comb can be used. Several attempts may have to be made before you are satisfied with the tightness.

By following steps 6 and 7 you create a tabby, or plain, weave because you have taken the weft under and over the warp. You have now begun to form the fabric, and you'll be surprised at how fast the weaving will progress. You can weave solid areas or stripes, or go about it in a hit-or-miss fashion by mixing materials. Even the texture may be varied by using different fabrics or materials such as fur, ribbons, and ropes.

As an alternative to the tabby, you may want to use the Ghiordes knot with pieces of cut weft, as is done with the Rya rug, or you may decide to chain across the weft. The chain does for this weaving what the tabby does between the knotted rows of the Rya or Flossa rug. It is made in the same way that the chain stitch is made in embroidery (see page 67). The chain is usually worked from left to right with a needle or with the fingers. It makes a decorative stitch that incorporates the warp threads.

8. If your shuttle does not carry much material, you will need to add to it. Any additional strips can be sewed on with a machine, but a close backstitch can accomplish the same thing, and for only one seam it is simpler.

9. To remove the woven strip from the loom, clip the center pair of warp threads on one end and tie them securely against the edge of the woven part of the rug. To prevent strain, tie every other pair of threads by cutting the cords around each pair of nails and tying the ends together to create a sort of fringe. Anchor those in the corners first, to hold the rug taut while you tie the center threads. Always work from the center out to the sides. Finally tie the corner threads. You are now ready to rewarp your loom, and duplicate this strip, if you wish.

If there is a sufficient amount of warp left at the ends, you might make a braided or macramé finish. Another type of finish might be several rows of tabby woven across each end.

10. To make a carpet or a runner, strips made on this loom can be sewed together (Figure 19). If you plan to make a carpet, it is advisable to plan your weaving by distributing material in boxes so that the strips can be duplicated. When two strips are sewed together, the colors at the seams must match so that when the rug is finished, the general impression will be that it was done on a wide loom.

FIGURE 19   Runner made by sewing 3 rugs together end to end.

THE CARRIAGE WHEEL WHIRL

Most of the looms we have discussed have been rectangular looms. You can, however, create interesting circular items on a round loom such as the Carriage Wheel Whirl (Plate 6).

Materials

1. Almost any round frame such as a bicycle tire rim, a quilting loom, or an iron carriage wheel is suitable for this loom if it is firm and provides weaving space. The size of the finished rug is, of course, determined by the dimensions of the rim you choose to use.

2. Strips of soft wool or cotton provide the filler. If the material is heavy, cut the strips 1½ inches wide. If lightweight, cut them wider. Their length should equal the diameter of the frame plus 6 inches for sewing or pinning the ends to the rim.

Procedure

1. Place the rim you have selected on a table or a flat surface. Divide it into seven equal parts, or more if you have a very large rim. The marks should correspond to points A, B, C, D, E, F, G in Figure 20.

FIGURE 20 Placement of strips on the rim.

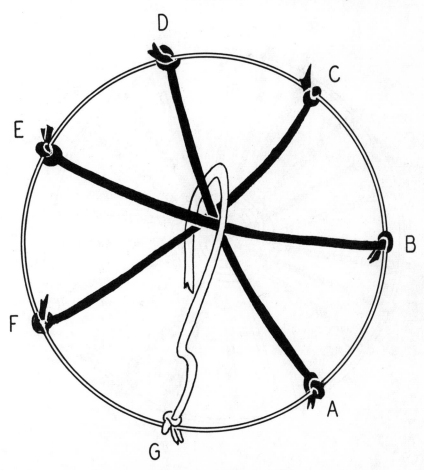

2. Fold in the edges of three of the strips. Fasten the first one between points A and D, the second one between B and E, and the third one between C and F.

3. A fourth strip of material that is longer than the first three is used as the weaver spoke, or spoke G. Mark it with chalk or thread for identification purposes and tie it between points A and F at G.

4. Tie the free end of the weaver spoke in a taut knot over all the other spokes in the center of the wheel. This knot will hold the spokes firmly together.

5. After tying the center knot, weave the end of tie G (Figure 21) around the center under F and over E, under D and over C, under B and over A, under G. Now alternate, weaving the end of tie G *over* F and *under* E, *over* D and *under* C, *over* B and *under* A, *over* G. Alternate again, weaving *under* F and *over* E, etc., stopping at G.

6. Next add two spokes in each arc between the original spokes. Start at the right of F and continue around. Use strips long enough to reach the G strand in the center and to come back again to the rim, forming a V (Figure 21). Pin each of them securely on the rim.

FIGURE 21 Circular weaving.

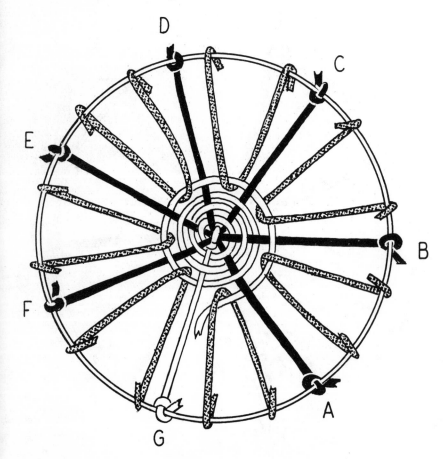

Woven by Frieda Z. Tuinsma
Photo by Lloyd Rule Studios

PLATE 1 Rya rug.

PLATE 2 Flossa rug designed and woven by Marilyn Léon.

PLATE 3 Hooked rug.

Made by Winifred Hare

Courtesy of the International Folk Art Museum, Sante Fe, N. M.
Photo by James B. De Korne

7. Take strand G and weave it around the center through the original spokes and the new spokes. If the weaver strand has become too short, add to it.

8. Add still another series of spokes, as you did in Step 6. If the weaving area is becoming crowded, you may add single spokes instead of the double ones you have been using. If using a single spoke, fold it over and hand-sew it in the center. It can then be pulled to the rim and fastened.

9. Continue weaving until the entire area is filled and then unfasten the strips.

10. There are several ways that this circular woven rug can be finished. Backstitch around the edge, or clip the spoke ends and form a fringe (Figure 22). Or you can clip the ends close to the rug and bind them. If you want a braided edge, make several braids and lace them together. Sew a piece of burlap onto the back of the rug so that it extends several inches beyond the the edge. This burlap will support the braid.

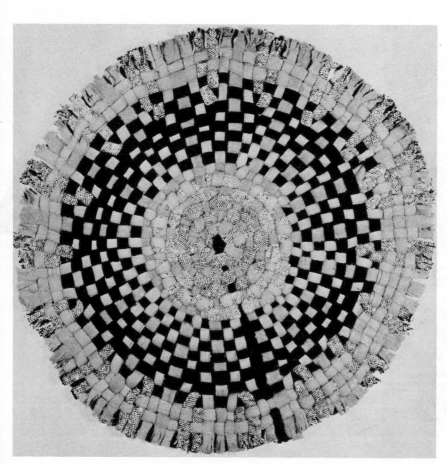

FIGURE 22 Completed rug with fringed edge.

4

PLAITED, CROCHETED, AND SHIRRED RUGS

THE PLAITED RUG

A plaited rug is made of very fine strips of cotton. After the strips are plaited, they are sewed together in spiral fashion with fine stitches. The result is what was formerly called a rag rug.

You may be surprised to see that the plaited rug has its own classification and is not listed under woven or braided rugs. This is because it is actually woven with the fingers rather than on a loom, and it is lighter in weight and thinner than a braided rug. It is most often made of cotton rather than wool and is never made room size. Why is it included in this book? Mainly because plaiting has a number of uses other than its use in a rug. Although the plaited rug is never as firm or as durable as the three-strand braided rug or the woven rugs, its braids make a beautiful trim which can be added to many other items, depending on the material that is plaited. Because it is a flat rather than a round and hard braid, it is suitable for lampshades and sweaters, and as appliquéd trim on a rug or a hanging where it can add a banded decoration.

Materials

1. Cut five strips of material 1½ inches wide and not more than about 1 yard long. This makes interlacing easier.

PLATE 4 *Summer and Winter*, a wall hanging woven on a harness loom.

Woven by Frieda Z. Tuinsma
Photo by Lloyd Rule Studios

PLATE 5 Guatemalan girl at a backstrap loom.

Photo by O. Marinoff

PLATE 6 Carriage wheel whirl.
Photo by Lloyd Rule Studios

PLATE 7 Shirred rug.
Made by Catherine Downing
Photo by Lloyd Rule Studios

Vary the lengths of the strips slightly to produce a flatter finished surface. This difference in length will mean that the seams will be staggered when additional material is sewed onto the strips to extend them as you plait. Fold the edges under and baste or press them down with an iron.

2. Safety pin.

Procedure

1. Slip the five prepared strands onto a safety pin with the folds facing to the left. It is just as simple to use more strips but it takes a little more time.

2. Begin to plait on the right (always work from right to left). As in Figure 23, take strip number 1 over 2, under 3, over 4, and under 5. Leave it in a horizontal position off to the left. Pin it in place until you have a good start.

3. Take strip number 2 over 3, under 4, over 5, and under 1. Leave number 2 in the horizontal position. Note that number 1 is no longer in a horizontal position.

4. Weave number 3 to the left over 4, under 5, over 1, under 2 and leave number 3 in the horizontal position in place of 2.

5. Number 4 now becomes the weaver strip. Take it over 5,

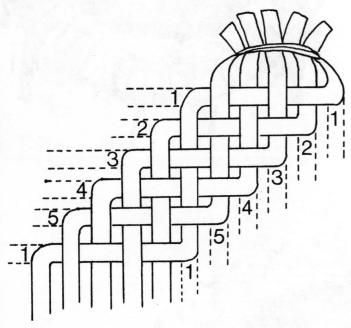

FIGURE 23 Plaiting.

under 1, over 2, under 3, and leave 4 in the horizontal place.

6. Number 5, now the weaver, goes over 1, under 2, over 3, and under 4 into the horizontal location.

7. Continue plaiting in this manner. Use a sewing machine to add additional material to the strips when they need to be lengthened, or sew it on by hand with fine stitches.

8. If you are making trim, plait the exact amount or length you will need for its particular location. It can be applied with invisible stitching or put on with cloth adhesive or milliner's glue.

9. More preparation is involved in making a rug. Have yards and yards of material prepared. Lay the strip on a flat surface where you can leave it. Moisten your hands and begin to shape the center of your rug pinning it in a circular position. Do not work more than a foot in diameter. Allow this to dry and then hand-sew it with tight stitches, hiding them as best you can.

10. Continue until your rug is nearly completed. The tail end should be trimmed. Taper it to a thinness that will let it become quite inconspicuous against the last row.

11. If you wish to finish your rug with a completed strip, read Chapter 5 on braided rugs. Measure the distance around your rug and tuck in the edges of your strips, sewing them together. Plait another strip equal to the diameter of the rug and sew the ends together. Drop this braceletlike ring around your rug, pin it in many places, and sew it to the rug. A thin pad placed underneath the plaited rug makes it more serviceable.

THE CROCHETED RUG

Quickly and easily made, the crocheted rug is one of America's favorite throw rugs for the kitchen, dining room, bedroom, or bath. It can be crocheted with cotton or woolen strips from new material, sewing scraps, or old garments. It costs almost nothing. A wooden needle, Size 19, or a metal J-needle makes a large, fast stitch that enables you to have a crocheted rug in an amazingly short time.

Design

There is a wide range of designs and patterns for crocheted rugs. If you crochet, you can make anything you want; if you do not

PLATE 8 Braided rug.

PLATE 9 Braided stair treads.

Photo by Lloyd Rule Studios

PLATE 10 Braided rug.

know how, you can learn very quickly by practicing on a large needle.

Materials

1. Prepare your material by cutting strips about an inch wide. Sew these together on a machine and roll them into balls. Some people prefer to have strips cut on the bias, while others want them cut on the straight of the material. The bias cut will crochet more easily, but the straight strips simplify turning in the edges.
2. To make the rag balls, use solid-color material. Short lengths sewed together can be used to make the hit-or-miss rug. For a banded rug, have balls of plain colors made up which you may distribute through the rug as you choose.
3. A Size 19 wooden needle or a metal J-needle.

Procedure

1. For an oval rug, crochet a chain one-third the length of the finished rug. If the rug is to be 36 inches long, the center will be 12 inches long. When this chain is made, single-crochet all around it. Continue around and around. You will need to add stitches to complete the rug. There is no rule for determining how many stitches should be added or just when to add them. How tightly you crochet and how heavy your strips are will determine the result. Stitches are added by returning to each hole twice and then crocheting it.

   It is important to place a pin or mark where you add stitches. Stitches added to either side of the center and on each end should match. Do not add stitches at the same point on each successive round; stagger them, but be sure that they match on either side of the rug or the completed rug will be lopsided.
2. Even if a crocheted rug is well made, it may have surplus material in the center after it has been washed. Don't worry about this. Place your rug on a flat surface and pat it flat. Take a cup of thin starch and spread it over the rug's surface with your palm. When the rug dries, it will be flat and resistant to soil, dog hair, and grease.

THE CROCHETED SHIRRED RUG (Plate 7)

The sturdy crocheted shirred rug is very suitable for a contemporary setting. Made from shirred strips of woolen material crocheted together, these rugs can be interesting as large or small floor pieces. Attractive stair treads can be made if the strips are not cut so wide that they make the treads too thick.

Design

A color scheme and a design can be planned before you start, or you can more or less let the design "happen" as you go along. If you are not looking for specific colors, the hit-or-miss variety of design is naturally the easiest, since the rug can be made from varying lengths of woolen pieces which are easily available.

Materials

1. The needle used for making this rug is 10 or 12 inches long with a point on one end and a crochet hook on the other. If this needle is not available, substitute an afghan needle and file the end opposite the hook to a point.
2. Cut strips of woolen material ¾ inch wide and 12 to 18 inches long, depending on the thickness of the material. Cut on the straight of the material or on the bias. The width determines the thickness of the rug.
3. A ball of twine or crochet thread that is strong enough to make a firm rug.

Procedure

1. Gather one strip of wool into 5/8-inch folds and slide these over the needle point toward the hook end.
2. Make a slip knot over the crochet hook with twine or crochet thread and make a chain stitch. Pick up the stitch, pull it through the slip knot, and slide one fold of the wool off the hook.
3. Continue to chain stitch in the same manner until the first strip of wool is completely shirred. Then slide the next woolen strip over the pointed end of the needle and continue to chain-stitch the folds together.
4. When enough strips have been chained together to form the center of the rug, start to increase the size of the rug by sliding a new folded woolen strip onto the needle. From this point, all the work is done by single crocheting into each stitch between the folds. Pull the stitch through the wool with each single crochet and slip the fold of wool off the hook. Always keep the thread taut and make your work even and tight to insure a firm rug.
5. When one strip has been single-crocheted to the center, slide a new strip onto the needle and continue around,

PLATE 11 Carpet-piece rug.

Assembled by Rebecca Moyer
Photo by Lloyd Rule Studios

PLATE 12 Fur rug.

PLATE 13 Cross-stitch sampler.

Photo by Lloyd Rule Studios

Loaned by Frances Sargent
Photo by Lloyd Rule Studios

PLATE 14 Open cross-stitched rug.

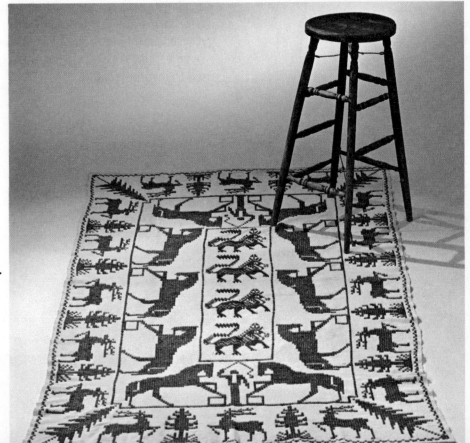

turning the work when necessary. On the curves increase with additional stitches to keep the rug flat. Notice that every time a strip is used up a a new one is added.

6. As you work around the center of the rug and as the rug increases in size, it will be more and more difficult to locate the stitches hidden between the folds. Continue to single-crochet into each stitch, slipping off the folds of wool each time until your rug is completed. As you work, you will develop a rhythm and your work will become easier and easier. When the rug is completed, tie a secure knot and clip the thread. The tail of wool left over can be hand-sewed against the edge of the rug.

7. If you should ever wish to make the rug larger (even after using it), single-crochet additional strips into position as you did before.

THE KNITTED SHIRRED RUG

If you know how to knit, you might like to make a knitted shirred rug instead of the crocheted version. It uses smaller pieces of material and is incorporated into the knitting after stitches have been cast on. It makes a very soft and fluffy rug.

THE HAND-SEWED SHIRRED RUG

If you do not crochet or knit, or if you just want to make a shirred rug by sewing, you can use a method such as that described for crocheting. As with crocheted rugs, your strips may be cut on the straight or on the bias. The latter produces an especially good result and helps the material to curve better. These strips are gathered with running stitches; once they are gathered, sew them together in rows forming a weblike base, or woven effect. A good carpet warp or mattress twine should be used to insure strength.

5

BRAIDED RUGS

BASIC PROCEDURES

The braided rug is not only versatile in design, it is also very strong and durable. Its braids are made of woolen strips laced together in such a way that it never buckles or loses its shape.

History tells us little of the braided rug until it was more or less perfected and brought into prominence by New Englanders. Although we usually associate braided rugs with Early American homes, the first braided rug was actually a mat made by the Egyptians from some variety of rushes. Even the caveman made primitive mats which served as a bed by night and a seat by day, lending warmth and decoration to his sparse surroundings. The earliest recorded floor coverings used by the Pilgrims were corn-husk mats braided by the colonists. Reproductions of these early mats are displayed in picturesque Williamsburg.

The braided rug craft has spread so extensively that if you do not want to make your own rugs, you may have an all-wool rug made to order in the size, design, and color of your choice. The price of a 9 x 12 rug varies from seven hundred to as much as one thousand dollars. What was once a hobby has become a profitable business for many enthusiasts. Some professionals employ many helpers to keep their orders filled. Still, the

PLATE 15 Colcha embroidery by Rebecca James

Courtesy of the International Folk Art Museum, Santa Fe, N. M.
Photo by James B. De Korne

greatest proof of the charm of these rugs is that the majority of them are made by amateurs.

Rugmakers frequently ask how long it will take to make a room-sized rug. A great deal depends on the amount of time you have to work on it. When you are eager to make your own rug, you can readily find time you didn't realize was available. You will be surprised how many five-, ten-, and fifteen-minute periods you may use if the materials are cut and ready to braid. How fast you work and your dexterity in braiding and sewing will naturally be determining factors in how long it takes to complete the rug. Those with experience can make a rug in several months, but a beginner, however ambitious, should plan on a year for a 9 x 12 rug (Figure 24). It is better to make a small rug first. In that way you can master the

FIGURE 24 This center is the beginning of a 9 x 12 rug. Yards of braiding are ready to be joined and laced on.

technique and thereby enable yourself to attempt a room-sized rug without any difficulty.

Design

The first factors to be considered are the location, size, and shape of your rug. You would not select the same size rug for a bedroom as you would for a living room, nor the same shaped rug for a hall as for a den. In planning your rug, keep its location in mind.

A room-sized rug, always very attractive, tends to make a room appear larger. A round rather than an oval rug is better in a square room. But the long room looks better with an oval or rectangularly shaped rug. If your living room is very long and narrow, three small rugs will help to camouflage its length.

In decorating nothing is more important than color. You will enjoy combining greens, yellows, browns, and various shades of blue and rose. Tweeds make interesting contrast braids and many rugmakers feel that a rug without them loses much of its beauty. The choice of color will be influenced by the rug's location: warm colors for rooms with northern exposure, cooler hues for sunny rooms. Even the wood in your furniture plays a part in the color scheme. Pine, maple, and light cherry seem to call for shades of rust, red, yellow, and green. Walnut, mahogany, and dark cherries are better with plum shades, roses, grays, and blues.

Rugs in many shades of one color are very beautiful; gathering the material for such rugs can be interesting, too.

In deciding what colors to work into your rug, look at your slipcovers, your draperies, and that large picture on the wall. Pick out the background colors and use the more striking shades as accents. With hit-or-miss rugs almost anything can be used.

Those who like contemporary designs may find a style among the braided rugs which will follow the simple lines of their furniture as well as complement the nubby cotton upholstery fabrics in their homes. Color, as in all decoration, is an important factor which can be used to make different periods complement one another. How versatile a rug can be is limited only by your own imagination, artistry, and determination, for there are many different ways of combining colors.

A banded rug may be made of hit-or-miss colors in any combination. A braid in which all three strands are the same color adds the finishing touch to this rug and gives a banded or accented look.

The hit-or-miss rug is satisfying to make after another rug has been completed and only the leftover colors are available. Short pieces, 4-6 inches long are sewed together on the bias to make the continuous strips. After they are braided, they form a very attractive, more or less variegated, pattern. If you are making a large rug, solid bandings or a deep border of a solid color will help to tie the rug into the color scheme. Most individual and interesting rugs can be made this way.

The shaded rug requires material of the right colors. This style uses all shades of a color from the lightest to the deepest. It may progress from dark to light or vice versa in a sunburst effect. No two people combine their colors in the same order or intensity. The result reflects individual taste.

Materials

1. Good sources for new woolens are numerous. Use pieces left over from your own sewing or from that of your friends. Visit mill-end stores and woolen mills that have coat remnants, blanket ends, and sample swatches. Remnants are available in dry goods stores.

2. If you are going to make a rug from old woolens, you can find good used material in old garments or blankets at such places as Goodwill Industries, the Veterans' Foundation, the Salvation Army, and Catholic Charities. Other splendid sources for used woolens are rummage sales, small thrift shops, estate sales, and army stores where army and navy blankets are available. These are excellent for dyeing dark green or brown.

3. Although it may be difficult to collect all-wool material, the softness of color, the wearing qualities, and the ease with which it braids and laces makes the search worthwhile. A heavy, soft, and firm material such as a camel's hair coat is best for firm, even braids. Do not use wiry or harsh cloth. A challis or flannel is too thin for the beginner because since it must be a wider strip, it tends to get extra folds and creases as you braid. Do not select material which takes a firm crease, such as men's suits of a hard weave. For example, a man's gabardine or tropical worsted suit is not good to use; it is too wiry and stiff and would result in a braid with creases which will catch dirt and make it wear out faster.

   Avoid use of materials with overshots in the weave such as some tweeds have; these wear out very quickly. Look for tightness and firmness as well as closeness of weave, comparable to the material in an army blanket.

4. The amount of material needed will depend somewhat on the type of material you are using. For example, camel's hair coats and blankets work up quickly, making a lighter rug than one made of remnants from some woolen mills, men's overcoats, or even most women's coats.

Like many rugmakers, you probably will not buy all the material needed for a large rug at one time. It is difficult to say how much of any one color might be required by weight unless you have decided on the proportion of each color to be used. For example, if you were making a 70-pound 9 x 12 oval rug with one-third in shades of green, one-third in shades of brown, one-sixth in yellows, and one-sixth in reds, you would have a very good idea of the amount you would need. If the amount of wool you have is limited, it is advisable to work out the color distribution beforehand. Depleting your color supply might mean that you would not be able to locate the shade you need later.

After weighing a number of braided rugs, the following weight figures were obtained. Weights may vary because materials are not uniform, but these estimates will give you an idea of what will be needed in poundage to complete a rug:

> 31 x 26 inches requires 4-1/8 pounds.
> 42 x 27 inches requires 6 pounds.
> 5 x 7 feet requires 23 pounds.
> 9 x 12 feet requires 70 pounds.

5. Tools and equipment:
> Large darning needle.
> Thimble.
> Safety pins.
> Sack needle (blunt end for lacing braids together) or a large round-end canvas or tapestry rug needle.
> Upholsterer's flax, sewing twine for lacing, or mattress twine.
> Rubber bands.
> Tailor's chalk.
> Yardstick.
> Sewing machine, unless you wish to sew firmly by hand.
> Scissors.

Preparation of Materials

1. Before washing used materials, shake them free of dust, remove buttons, linings, pockets, belts, and collars, and rip

out all seams. Wash the material in lukewarm soapy water in the washing machine and rinse several times without changing the temperature of the water. Dry thoroughly.

2. Test for bleeding. If your material has faded in the process of washing, you must repeat the process several times. If the water isn't clear in the last wash, the material will fade. You must set your color, if possible; if not, discard the fabric.

3. Dyeing materials is generally more expensive than finding material in the desired colors. However, in order to continue a rug when a color is not available, it is frequently necessary to dye. Regardless of the method you use—open kettle on the stove or automatic washer—be sure that the material is clean and that the water is hot enough. Automatic washers require at least 150 degrees. For good results, don't overload your container. Use a recognized brand of dye and be sure to have a sufficient amount on hand to do the job. Follow directions on the packages of dye or read the manual of your automatic washer under "dye."

4. To determine the width of the strips to be used in your braid, follow this procedure before tearing any strips: Roll the edge of a piece of material lengthwise until you have a ropelike, cylindrical form of sufficient bulk to make one strand, or one-third of the total braid. The width of the portion rolled, when opened and measured, gives the width of the strip to be cut. It may take as much as 3 inches of a soft material such as flannel to form the complementary strand to camel's hair, which may require for its width 1 or 1½ inches, depending on its thickness. If the cylindrical strands are all kept the same size, regardless of weight, the result will be a uniform braid.

   Make a sample braid before you tear your material. This will help determine what the thickness and width of the final braid will be. Some prefer a braid 2 inches wide, but more prefer the "near" inch, which is easier to handle.

   Do not cut material if it is possible to tear it. Tearing is not only quicker and easier, but it is also more accurate.

5. To join the torn strips, place the right sides together at right angles (Figure 25). Machine-stitch diagonally across from A to B. Trim the corner away, making a small seam (Figure 26) which will be easily hidden when included in the braid.

   If you do not have a sewing machine, these strips may be sewed together by hand. Keep the stitches very small,

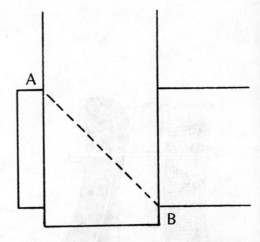

FIGURE 25 Joining strips for a braided rug.

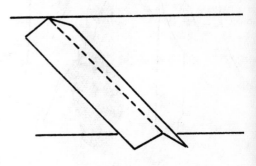

FIGURE 26 Seam of joined strips.

FIGURE 27 Three strands attached to safety pin for braiding.

FIGURE 28 Making the braid.

with a frequent backstitch to make the seam more permanent.

6. Before braiding be sure that you do not press or iron folded-in edges of the strands. The braid should be firm and round rather than flat and soft. Also, do not sew the edges of the strands together.

Braiding

1. When beginning to braid, do not let anyone hold the end of your braid. This stretches the braid and makes the rug less firm. It also forms the bad habit of anchoring the braid which is not always convenient to do. Don't pin the end to a chair, a couch, or give it support in any way. A tight, plump, and firm braid is obtained by pushing back against the previously formed portion of braid rather than by pulling.

2. After getting all material together and making yourself comfortable, take three strands of material. A three-color combination, such as the tweed, white, and black in the illustrations, is a great help to a beginner. Fold the outside edges of each strand toward the center; then fold in half. This leaves two folded edges together at the left and hides all raw edges of the material inside the strand or tube. Keep the folds of all three tubes to your left. Place the three tubes together, one on top of the other, on a heavy safety pin (Figure 27); or hold them together with a rubber band. The safety pin or rubber band is easily removed later.

3. Now you are ready to braid. Hold the three strands firmly in your hands, not supported by anything or anyone (Figure 28):

   Take the black over the white toward the left.
   Take the tweed over the black toward the right.
   Take the white over the tweed toward the left.
   Take the black over the white toward the right.
   Take the tweed over the black toward the left.
   Take the white over the tweed toward the right.
   Take the black over the white toward the left.
   Take the tweed over the black toward the right, etc.

   It is not easy to hold the braid in your hands, but keep trying and take out any mistakes. Practice braiding and taking out many times until you have mastered the technique.

4. Remember, you want a round, firm type of braid that will resist wear, not a soft, loose braid in which one piece of material is merely placed over the other. Again, take out any mistakes as they appear, since they will later mar the finished rug. If there is an extra crease or an uneven look,

take it out. Creases or folds on the top or underside of the braid show that the strands have become too wide. Narrow them by folding the edges more tightly. This may be done in the left fold from the top or from the underside.

Check both the top and bottom surfaces for even workmanship. One side must be as perfect as the other. By avoiding creases you will prevent the accumulation of dust and dirt which make a rug wear out faster. When braiding, do not have the third strip of any braid yards and yards long, as this causes braids to become tangled and hence slows the work.

5. Check your braids for folds on the left side. If you see a continuous line made by these folds, then everything is all right. This left edge should resemble a seam in appearance.

THE OVAL RUG

Now that you have learned to braid, you can start to make a beautiful, reversible, and useful braided rug which will last a lifetime (Plate 8). The method used to join the braids to make an oval rug is called the Completed Braid Method, a technique that was originated by the author and has been followed successfully by hundreds of rugmakers. In this method the two ends of a braid are joined together on the sewing machine. The braid is actually completed before it becomes a part of the rug thereby providing more working length while joining the ends. The use of a sewing machine shortens the time for joining and makes stronger braids. If you have forty braids in the rug, there will be forty joinings.

There are several advantages to this method. If the rug should wear out in any part, or if you should wish to change colors in the center or any section, parts may be easily removed. Moreover, if you want to braid away from home when your rug has become too large to carry with you, braiding materials may be assembled and taken any place you go.

The closed braid may be used to make a small or a room-sized rug. It is serviceable, will not buckle or cup; and if large enough, it gives a carpeted effect. This method may be used for hall runners or stair treads as well (Figure 29 and Plate 9).

Joining the Braids

1. It is important to measure the braid lengths correctly. As a rug increases in size, each succeeding braid will naturally be longer than the previous one. To determine how much this increase in length must be, multiply the braid's width by 6. For example, if the previous braid was 5 feet long and 1 inch wide, it should be followed by a braid 5 feet 6 inches long. This increase in the braid's length remains constant

FIGURE 29 Stair treads made by the Completed Braid Method.

FIGURE 30 *(left)* Joining one strand of the braids together.

FIGURE 31 *(right)* Two strands are joined.

FIGURE 32 *(left)* The final strand is in position, ready to be stitched.

FIGURE 33 *(right)* The final strand is stitched.

regardless of how large the rug may grow. As a general rule to determine the length of each successive braid, add to the *length* of the preceding braid its *width* multiplied by 6.

2. Before the braid is used in the rug, however, the ends of each braid must be joined together. This is done by sewing the strands on each end to their corresponding strands. If the braid has three different colors, you will have no real difficulty in joining the strands. Simply join strands of the same color.

3. To join the strands — for instance, the tweed ones in the illustrations — cut them on the bias so that they will match. Cut the material right side up from the lower left-hand corner to the upper right. It is not necessary to make any allowance for seams. However, best results are obtained if the first strip joined is a little shorter than the next two since they have a slightly greater distance to go.

4. With the right sides of the first strip together, stitch a small seam on the sewing machine (Figure 30). Be sure that the strands are not twisted. Take care that the tweed strand, for example, comes over a white from both ends of the braid and that the seam is on the inside. Do the same with the next set of strips (Figure 31).

5. If your braid contains strands of the same color, there is a problem determining just which strands should be joined together. Here the only procedure is to study the rhythm of the braid. Study the way the strands "flow." After you have studied the braid and know what you are going to do, it is a good idea to unbraid about 5 inches of the strand to give yourself more working space.

6. After two of the strands have been joined, braid the final strand down through. Before you make the last seam, be sure the order of the strands is correct, or the same as it was in the braid. If everything is in its correct position, cut the final strips on the bias and pull them tightly (Figure 32). Stitch (Figure 33).

7. If the last part of the braid is not as symmetrical as it should be, pull it around with your fingers to make it uniform. After some practice, this step will not be necessary.

Forming the Rug's Center

1. If you want to make an oval rug 4 x 6 feet, the center should be 2 feet long. This is the difference between the length and the width of the finished rug. Make a braid 4 feet long, and join the ends to make it 2 feet long. This could be the center for a rug 5 x 7, 6 x 8, or 2 x 5.

2. Pin the braid together (Figure 34); then thread the sack needle with lacing twine and attach the twine by tying a slip knot on the inside of an end strand (Figure 35). In the center the braids do not form the V that makes lacing from the underside so simple. Instead, lacing must come from the top on one side and from underneath on the other braid.

3. Take the needle into the top braid under the white strand (Figure 36). Hide the twine between the tweed and the white.

4. Drop to the lower braid and from the top go under the black strand.

5. Go across to the top braid under the tweed. Slip the cord against the tweed and the black.

6. In the lower braid, lace from the top under the tweed.

7. Move to the upper row. Go under the black, letting the cord hide against the black and the white.

8. In the lower row from the top, lace under the white.

9. In the upper braid, lace under the white. Slide the cord against the tweed hiding it.

10. In the lower braid from the top, go under the black.

11. In the upper braid, go under the tweed. Hide the cord between the tweed and the black.

12. In the lower braid from the top, go under the tweed. Continue lacing through the center braid until it is finished. If you have a long thread left, leave it uncut to use later. The second braid can be laced on with this cord.

FIGURE 34 Completed braid is sewed together and pinned to form the center for an oval rug.

FIGURE 35 Fasten the twine with a slip knot before starting to lace.

FIGURE 36 Start lacing by bringing needle under white strand of top braid.

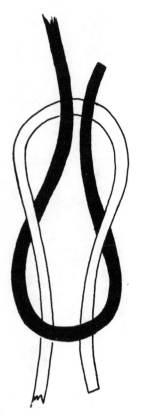

FIGURE 37 Use a square knot to attach additional twine.

Lacing on the Second Braid

1. Lay the completed braid around the laced center braid. Ease the braid into position and pin it in place with safety pins. Be sure the folds of the braid are against the center braid, not to the outside. Also, for faster, more perfect lacing, match the braids so that they form the V.

2. Use the threaded needle left from the first braid, if possible. Bring the needle into the second braid, coming from underneath. Pull the thread tightly, hiding it between the strands.

3. Go into the center braid. From underneath, lace through to the top again, hiding the cord. This lacing continues until the second braid is laced onto the center. On the ends of the oval rug you may need to skip a strand. This is like adding a stitch in crocheting.

4. After lacing back and forth from the center to the outside braid and pulling it up close, you will begin to see a blended effect as each braid loses its identity. If any threads show, take the braids in your fingers and jiggle them back and forth to conceal these threads.

5. When you need a new thread, tie a new piece on to 4 inches of the old piece with a square knot (Figure 37).

6. When you reach the point at which you began lacing, go in and out, lacing back and forth covering your old path. Doubling back will prevent any looseness.

FIGURE 38 The braid is spiraled to begin the center of a round rug.

THE ROUND RUG

Both the oval and round rugs are traditional styles. They complement the old furniture so cherished by antique lovers and lend authenticity to these antique settings (Plate 10).

Although spiraling is not an accepted method for rug-making in this book, a small center can be started this way. Use no more than three to five braids, and form them into a spiral pattern (Figure 38). When you finish, taper the end of the braid, making a slender tail. Braided tightly together, the end fits snugly against the body of the rug. If properly done, this center section will form an almost perfect circle.

Now braids can be added, using the Completed Braid Method. This rug will never cup or make problems. The color can be worked out in a hit-or-miss style or in a banded and shaded pattern.

THE CHAIN RUG

In this rug (Figure 39), any number of circles or ovals are placed in one continuous chain, depending on the length you want your rug or runner to be. The circles are sewed firmly together in a chain to form the center of the rug. Then the closed braid is used to surround the circles. Do not use more than three or four braids, for too many will eliminate the scalloped effect of the rug. It is important to keep the circles in a straight line, and to force the braid into the V where the circles meet.

FIGURE 39 The chain rug.

FIGURE 40 Circles 'round a circle.

COMBINATION OF CIRCLES

Another method for making an unusual rug is to line up three or more rows of circles and sew them together where they touch. These rows can then be encircled with braids. There will be openings between circles, but these are not at all objectionable if your circles are as close together as possible. A room-sized rug of this plan, using three or more circles across, is exceptionally lovely.

If you cannot work the braided circles very closely together, do not attempt this rug. Use the variation of this pattern instead. In the variation, the openings are filled in with short braids whose ends have each been whipped closed. The braids are forced into the openings and made to take whatever shape is needed to fill the opening left between the circles: a V, a U, or just a short curved piece. Sew these braids in with heavy thread. Make these additions carefully and thoughtfully so that the added portions will be symmetrical in the overall pattern they help to create.

CIRCLES 'ROUND A CIRCLE

Still another variation (Figure 40) is a rug with a circle in the center surrounded by other circles. Braids may be added to follow the scalloped outline of the circles. The braids add as much in decorative value as they do in extra stability. If enough of these braids are used the rug will become round. If all circles are the same size, it will take six to surround the one in the center. You can vary this pattern with a large circle in the center surrounded by smaller ones and a completed braid.

RECTANGULAR RUG A

The rectangular rug has many design possibilities. A rug 3 feet wide and 5 feet long will use 36 1-inch braids. These braids, each 5 feet long and 1 inch wide, are placed parallel to one another and laced together (Figure 41). To finish, use scissors to clip the ends and make a fringe, or turn in the ends of each braid and overcast. If you want a bound edge or a facing, use a wide bias strip of matching material.

RECTANGULAR RUG B

The rectangular rug (Figure 42) is formed in the same manner as Rug A. The difference is the use of an additional braid or braids, which are joined, placed around the entire rug, and sewed on as a border. For a larger rug any number of these braids may be added.

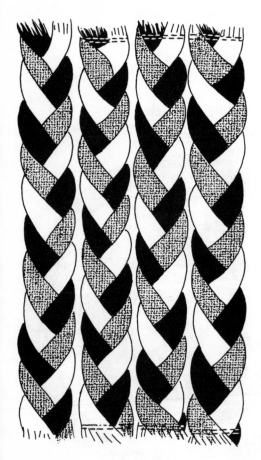

FIGURE 41 Rectangular Rug A.

RECTANGULAR RUG C

A very effective rectangular rug (Figure 43) is one which begins with a braid 8-½ feet long placed diagonally across the center, corner to corner. Make the rest of the braids in pairs that are progressively smaller as they near the corners. Lace a braid first on the one side of the center braid, then on the other, continuing to add braids until the rug has been completed. The last ones will be only 1 inch long. Placing a braid around the outside of the rug will make it more attractive and sturdier.

RECTANGULAR RUG D

A fourth rug with rectangular lines (Figure 44) can be made by using a continuous braid. It has no joinings. Start at what will be the upper right-hand corner of the finished rug. The end of this braid curves down slightly where it begins. Draw the braid to what will be the upper left-hand corner of the completed rug, curve it around back to the right side. Sew it into position under the first braid to form the second braid. Before your braid becomes too short, add new strips whose ends have been cut on the bias and sewed together on the machine. When making this rug, it is important that the braids are in a straight line and that the turns on the right and left sides are kept even.

FIGURE 42 Rectangular Rug B.

FIGURE 43 Rectangular Rug C.

FIGURE 44 Rectangular Rug D.

THE ZIGZAG RUG

The zigzag rug (Figure 45) should not be undertaken by the amateur. Careful workmanship is needed to insure symmetry. The following directions are for a zigzag rug which will measure 42 x 60 inches.

For best results, make a 42 x 60 inch rectangular frame. Place a 72-inch piece of 1 x 2 inch lumber diagonally from the upper right-hand corner to the lower left.

The Z is formed with a braid 156 inches, or 4-1/3 yards, long. Fasten the first end of the braid to the upper left-hand corner and carry the braid across to the upper right-hand corner (42 inches). Fasten it there. Then, form the diagonal by going to the lower left-hand corner, fasten the braid there, and finish by carrying it over to the lower right-hand corner.

Each side of the Z is filled in with V-shaped braids which are laced to one another. Be sure the braids run in the same direction before you lace. Be very particular, too, to see that each braid is fitted in closely against the other in the V or corner of the Z. Begin by lacing one braid onto the left side and then lacing a second braid onto the right side. Continue from side to side until the Z is filled in to make an even, well-balanced rug.

FIGURE 45 The zigzag rug.

FIGURE 46 The free-form rug.

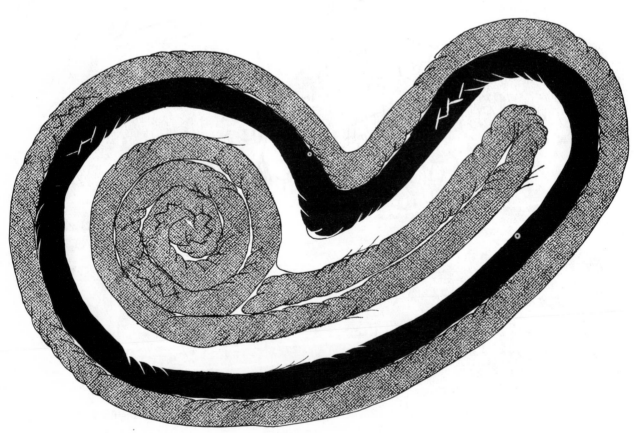

GETTING STARTED IN HANDMADE RUGS

THE FREE-FORM RUG

Start this rug (Figure 46) with a center made by spiraling a 1-1/8 inch wide braid seven times around. Instead of cutting the last braid short, let it extend 30 inches and turn back against itself until it reaches the original circle. Overcast the ends adjacent to the circle, and sew them firmly. Measure your next braid to go around this irregularly shaped center, join, pin to the center, and lace.

In braiding, be sure to maintain the line or shape desired. Are your braids running in the same direction so that you will be able to lace them together? If you continue to add fourteen braids, each 1-1/8 inches wide, each closed and then laced on, the completed rug should be about 74 inches long, 31 inches across the "tail," and 47 inches across the circle.

FIGURE 47 The half-circle rug.

THE HALF-CIRCLE RUG

The half-circle rug can be used in many locations. It goes well in front of a chest of drawers or a fireplace, beside a bed, or in an entrance hall.

In Figure 47 the method for making the half-circle rug is well illustrated. The first braid is placed in the center, and the size of the rug is determined by the number of additional braids. The edges are finished by firmly sewing the open ends together.

TRIANGULAR RUG

The triangular rug is made by using a 36-inch braid as the base of a triangle. Continue to lace braids, each shorter than the previous braid, one above the other, until the final point at the top is reached. Finish by tucking in the edges of the braids and sewing them together.

ENCLOSED TRIANGULAR RUG

After making a triangular rug, enclose the triangle with a braid or braids (Figure 48). This particular idea works very well for a large, even a room-sized, rug. If the braids are placed against each other properly, the braid that surrounds the original triangle can be laced on at the base. It must be sewed onto the other two sides, however, to give the rug a flat surface. Sewing on the surrounding braid is also a stronger method than lacing it to the ends of the braids in the original triangle.

STAIR TREADS (Plate 9)

Begin these small rugs (Figure 49) with a center 17 inches long made of a closed braid which is laced together through the center. To increase the tread to its proper size, add four more closed braids by lacing on one at a time around the center. For the best results, use woolen materials.

FIGURE 48 Enclosed triangular rug.

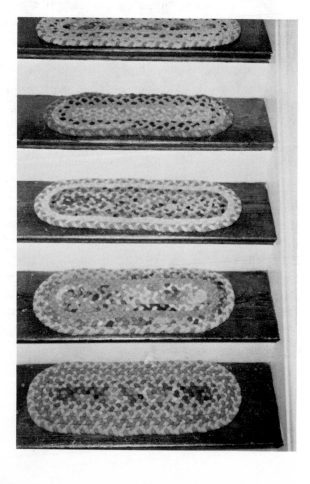

FIGURE 49 Stair treads.

6

QUICK AND EASY RUGS

CARPET-PIECE RUG (Plate 11)

A striking contemporary rug can be made from carpet pieces. Swatches, remnants, strips, and scraps from carpet installers can be made into useful and beautiful floor coverings. This rug can be assembled quickly, finished, and laid on the floor in hours after the materials have been gathered. It is simply unbelievable.

Design

The variety of shapes you will find will be a challenge to your imagination, offering a whole new range of ideas for rugs. The more squares and rectangles you use, the simpler your design will be. Unusual shapes, however, can be greater fun to put together, for they create a more interesting design. Experiment to decide where remnants should be placed on the foundation. They can be cut into circular pieces, odd shapes, or wide and narrow strips. Consider the size of the pieces you will have to fit together. Study the compatibility of various color combinations in order to get a bold presentation. Texture, too, should be kept in mind. The assortment of pieces — curly, long, short, clipped, shag, or even velvet — can be arranged to give a feeling of balance. Put them together to create an interesting design for the finished rug.

Materials

1. Obtain swatches and remnants from a carpet installer.
2. The foundation can be a heavy burlap or awning canvas.
3. Razor.
4. Grease pencil.
5. Adhesive.
6. Wrapping paper.

Procedure

1. Cut the foundation material to the size and shape that you want. Finish the edges with a 2-inch hem. Miter the corners to give a flat surface.
2. Experiment to decide where the remnants should be placed on the foundation. Consider the size, color, texture, and shape of the remnants.
3. Before cutting the pieces, make paper patterns.
4. With a grease pencil, mark around the patterns on the burlap or canvas background. Number the patterns and outlines to correspond. Remember to plan carefully so that you will use the material you have to the best advantage. Use the information you gathered from your trial-and-error experiments.
5. Next cut the carpet. This is not a difficult operation. Put the right side of the rug against the floor. Take a razor and cut on your pattern line between the wires or threads. Check to make sure that the pieces fit into their respective areas.
6. Spread heavy wrapping paper under the burlap or canvas. Carefully read the directions for using your adhesive and begin the task of attaching the carpet pieces to the foundation.
7. Start in the upper left-hand corner of the rug, handling only one section at a time. Put adhesive on the back of piece number 1 and lay it in the correct position. Pat and press it gently. Place the pattern piece on top and put books or some heavy object over the pattern to hold it firmly in place. Lay the second shape to the right of number 1 in the same manner.
8. Continue to anchor the other sections. Where remnants come together, brush the rug pile from one piece over the one next to it to hide the seams. When all the sections have been placed on your rug, allow it to dry completely.

A QUICK RUG

Here is another suggestion for families who are here today and gone tomorrow to a new home. Large carpet squares or rectangles can be put together with zippers or large hooks and eyes sewed onto a rug tape which can be applied to the back surfaces of the rug pieces. Either of these methods makes it possible to convert the rug for a smaller room with little effort.

THE FUR RUG

Many people like fur rugs (Plate 12) on their floors. They are soft to the touch and add a look of opulence to a room. Some buy new rugs in shops. Others make their own from discarded stoles and coats or by sewing smaller fur pieces together into a unique floor covering. If you wish to make a rug and don't have a coat, see what you can find at a thrift shop or a garage sale.

Design

If your rug is to be made from small fur sections which you have collected, plan how to place the various colors and textures. Scattering them often provides more interest. If the fur is all the same kind but the pieces are small, try to have the grain running the same way on each piece.

Materials

1. Choose one kind of animal skin or gather different types that can be combined. Check the condition of the fur. First check for moths and then test to see if the fur itself is loose by pulling not in one place but all over the coat. Next check the skin on the back of the fur. It must not be dry and hard, or crumbly — that is, rotting away from having been stored without "breathing" in a cedar chest.
2. Heavy brown felt in a shade most suitable for the rug.
3. Scissors.
4. Brown paper.
5. Wooden mallet.
6. Nylon or silk thread.

Procedure

1. If you are using fur from a stole or a coat, remove the lining, buttons, and sleeves.
2. Clean any dust and lint from the fur by running it through a dryer with no heat, only air. Or hang the fur

outside to air, and then brush it vigorously. Going over the entire surface with the nozzle of the vacuum cleaner is also an efficient cleaning method.

3. Clean the surface soil from the fur in any of the following ways:

   a. Lay the fur on a flat surface. Wash with a sudsy sponge and warm water. Remove suds and soil with clear water. Wipe dry with a turkish towel. If soil is still evident, repeat the cleaning.

   b. Some people like to dip the fur in lukewarm water. When clean, the fur is hung on a line to drip dry.

   c. If you do not wish to use water, mix cornmeal with only enough Thoro to give a moist consistency. Apply with the palm of the hand and work the meal through the surface. Remove the meal that adheres with a brush. This may be all the cleaning that is necessary if the dust has been removed first.

4. You can give a rich luster to both new and old fur by glazing. This can be done at home by placing a heavy brown paper over the fur and running a hot iron lightly over the paper. The results may surprise you.

5. Make a pattern that will utilize the fur to its best advantage and guide you in shaping your rug.

6. Cut the fur by placing the material fur side down against a hard, flat surface. Mark the path for cutting. With scissors, cut the skin, *not* the fur.

7. Sew and mend any tear by placing the furry surfaces face to face. With a short, fine needle and nylon or silk thread, sew the edges together. The stitches must be shallow and very close together. A tiny buttonhole stitch or a plain overcast may be used. Diamond or triangular shapes of fur join together with less trouble and are less conspicuous.

8. When the seams are all sewed, flatten them with a wooden mallet by placing them fur side down on the floor.

9. For the rug backing, make a paper pattern that follows the rug's contour but extends several inches beyond. Cut the brown felt. The edges can be scalloped or pinked before the fur is attached.

10. Sew the fur to the felt along its edge, using small, firm stitches.

7

BEWITCHING STITCHERY

THE NEEDLEPOINT RUG

This soft, warm-looking rug is made with heavy rug yarn on canvas, using a tapestry needle. It wears very well and should not be confused with needlepoint made of fine tapestry yarn. The needlepoint rug is suitable for any room. It may be used as a bedside rug, beautiful to see and walk on. Or, as with various small rugs, several pieces can be put together into a considerably larger rug.

Design

Although stores and mail-order houses sell kits that supply everything for making needlepoint rugs, you may want to make your own pattern. You can do it, too. The crossbars of the single canvas on which needlepoint rugs are made help in planning the size of the design and its placement.

The single-type rug canvas is not difficult to find. Decide on the size you want, buy it, and begin to plan. For simplicity, the beginner should select stripes, geometric, or conventional patterns. If you are more experienced, you may wish to do more complicated stylized designs of animals, birds, fruits, and flowers. In making your selection, keep your room's décor in mind. Consider what you expect your rug to contribute to the color scheme and to the mood you are creating. Read the directions for the half cross-stitch as well as for the continental stitch. After trying each, choose the stitch that you will use on your rug.

Materials

1. Single canvas.
2. Rug yarns from 100 percent wool, acrilan, rayon and cotton, or a wool and nylon blend are suitable for the filler.
3. A large tapestry or canvas needle.

The Half Cross-Stitch

The half cross-stitch is very simple to do. It takes less yarn than the continental stitch and is, therefore, less expensive.

1. Thread the needle with a piece of yarn no longer than 30 inches.
2. Use a piece of canvas for practice work.
3. Work from the left-hand lower corner. Bring the needle up through the canvas from underneath into point 1 (Figure 50), leaving a 1½-inch tail of yarn. Hold this tail with your hand so that you will cover and anchor it on the underside with the next few stitches.
4. . Take the needle diagonally across from 1 to 2. Take the needle under the bar and bring it up through 3. Move diagonally over to 4.
5. Return under the bar with the needle in a vertical position and come up into 5. Move diagonally over to 6 and then through 7 from underneath. After you have practiced the stitch and when you have your pattern in mind, begin on your rug.
6. If you have a design, begin to work on it first. Start at the left and go to the right. After the designs have been stitched, you can fill in the background.

The Continental Stitch

The continental stitch is really no more difficult to work than the half cross-stitch, but it is thicker. This means it will use more yarn, which will pad the back of the rug as heavily as the front.

1. Work with 27- or 30-inch lengths of yarn. Begin at the right side in the lower corner.
2. Bring the needle from beneath at point 1 (Figure 51), leaving a 1½-inch piece of yarn as a tail. This piece will disappear under the next two stitches on the wrong side.

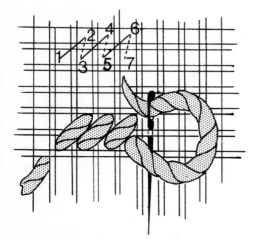

FIGURE 50 The half cross-stitch

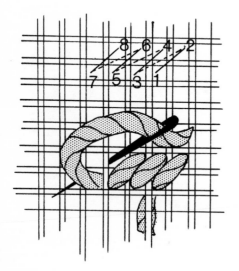

FIGURE 51 The continental stitch.

3. Go diagonally to the right into square 2. Come diagonally across from underneath, bringing the needle up at 3. Go diagonally across the top from 3 down through 4. This makes a second stitch.

4. Continue to the left side until the row is finished. From beneath, run the yarn back under the stitches on the wrong side and clip it off.

5. Return to the right side and stitch as you did in the beginning when you started your first row.

6. Now in the row above and to the right, bring the needle up through 2, diagonally over, down through 5. Come up from beneath at 4. Go diagonally into 7 and through to the underside. Continue with this same pattern to the left edge. Be sure the yarn is not drawn too tightly or twisted. In the continental, as in the half cross-stitch, it is best to work the designs first before starting the background.

After you have practiced both stitches on your canvas, you can easily choose the one you prefer. Since no frame is needed for this type of rug, it is "good company" to take with you anyplace you go. You can put your work on a table or hold it on your lap.

Blocking the Finished Rug

1. You may choose one of two surfaces on which to block your rug. The floor is a good place to work; so is an old table, if you have one large enough for your rug. In either case a piece of plastic covered by two thicknesses of an old sheet or bedspread will be needed.

2. Determine what size the finished rug is to be. Mark these measurements on the undercover.

3. Dip the rug into a tub of lukewarm (not hot) water until covered. This will dissolve the starch in the canvas. Do not wring or shake it as you take it gently from the bath. Pat the surface with turkish towels.

4. Place the rug on the marked sheet and stretch it to fit the dimensions. If the rug is on the floor, pin it in position with upholstery skewers or drapery pins. If you used an old table or wooden surface, use No. 6 upholstery tacks (inserted part way) or large thumbtacks. Pin down at the center of each edge; then continue pinning out to the corners, placing the pins a few inches apart.

5. Allow the rug to dry completely.

6. Hem or face down the edge with an overcast stitch, or use iron-on tape flat against the turned-down edges. Miter the corners on the tape to make a smooth surface.

THE CROSS-STITCH RUG

This rug is often referred to as child's play because it is made with one of the stitches first taught youngsters (Plate 13). Since it can be made so quickly and easily, it is appealing to the beginning craftsman. The cross-stitch rug is coarser than the needlepoint rug, and it works up faster.

Design

A pattern can be planned and the canvas colored to indicate placement of the yarn. Mark the fabric with dots that will serve as a pattern guide. Remember that the spacing of the dots will determine the size of the cross-stitches.

Materials

1. The foundation, or backing, can be made of canvas, as is the needlepoint rug. Very satisfactory results, however, have been obtained when a plain awning type canvas or a woolen fabric is used. After the size of the finished rug is determined, allow an extra 3 inches around the edge for a hem. This will be hand-sewed against the backing after the rug is completed.
2. For the best results the filler should be woolen rug yarn. There are many other yarns on the market today and it is interesting to see what is available at your local shops.
3. Tapestry needle.

Procedure

1. Thread a tapestry needle with 30 inches of yarn.
2. Starting at the left side, come from beneath at 1 (Figure 52,A). Leave a 1½-inch tail. Go diagonally to number 2 and put the needle through to the back. From underneath, move to number 3, bringing the needle through to the right side. Go diagonally to number 4 and drop down to number 5 from underneath. Bring the needle diagonally over to number 6. Go down through the canvas to the underside and come up at 7. Go diagonally to number 8. Continue to work across the canvas making these half cross-stitches.
3. To return from the right side, stitch over the same row in the opposite direction. Come to the surface at number 1 (Figure 52,B) and go diagonally to number 2. Move to number 3 from beneath. Come to the surface and go diagonally from 3 to 4. Go to number 5 from the underside. Come through to the top going diagonally from number 5

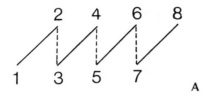

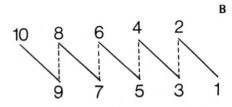

FIGURE 52 The cross-stitch.

to 6. Continue until you have a perfect row of crosses. Lock the thread and begin a new row at the left.

THE STAMPED MATERIAL CROSS-STITCH RUG

This rug (Plate 14) often seen in Central America, is the most common type for beginners. The coarse linen or sacking, used for the foundation, has dots or x's stamped on it to indicate where to make the stitches for the design. Another type of cross-stitch rug is made on a canvas with squares similar to that used for the Rya rug. A large bird, a geometric design, or even a horse can be drawn on the open cross-stitched rug. It is so-called because it looks like a piece of embroidery unlike the canvas-backed, cross-stitched rug that resembles woven cloth. The yarn supply used, the colors, and the open cross-stitch all contribute to making this rug very different from that done on needlepoint canvas. It is actually more fun to do, for it is more imaginative.

THE APPLIQUÉD RUG

The appliquéd rug, as the name implies, means that the designs are cut out and attached to the backing. There isn't a more decorative or a more "fun" rug to make; there is no limit to what you can do. The room in which it is to be placed should govern the design and color. Since this rug does not take hard wear, place it in an area where traffic is light.

Design

The design of an appliquéd rug might be large animals, figures, trees, stylized flowers, or even scenes. Nothing too detailed or too small should be used. This appliquéing venture is really for the craftsman with imagination who wishes to use everything that is available. You'll be delighted at the wonderful results you can get from appliquéing various materials onto one another. The appliquéd rug will enable you to use your ingenuity and will bring you much inner satisfaction.

Materials

1. Denim, burlap, or colored or neutral awning canvas is attractive for the background. Such heavy material will require machine stitching for the hem or binding and for the application of the designs. Heavy quality felt also works very well and it can be scalloped or finished with hand stitching. Heavy woolen fabric is another excellent material which is easy to work with either by hand or by machine.

2. Designs for the appliqué can be cut from a variety of materials. They must be closely woven and colorfast. The background to which they will be attached should be taken into consideration. The picture or design you are using might call for a mixture of materials such as leather, cotton, or even fur. You might want to use the fur to represent a little koala bear or squirrel. You can see why this rug is fun to do and why it stimulates all sorts of ideas.

3. Brown paper.

4. Grease pencil.

5. Cloth glue (optional).

Procedure

1. Draw the designs to be appliquéd on paper to make a pattern. Cut out the patterns and experiment by placing them on the background. They may have been perfect in your sketch, but now trial and error may be the solution to locating them in just the right place. When you are satisfied, mark around the patterns with a grease pencil. It is important to number the background figures to correspond to the patterns.

2. The designs can be machine sewed, especially if you have a machine with fancy stitches. If not, plain sewing hidden by colorful yarns in decorative hand stitchery may be used, even preferred. Designs may also be mounted with a cloth glue. Care must be taken to keep the adhesive from getting too near the edge. Hard glue is almost impossible to penetrate with a needle.

3. The edge of the design can also be turned under and basted down. Or a raw edge can be left and finished with a buttonhole, blanket, or satin stitch. Worked closely together, any of these add decorative value and prevent raveling.

THE CREWEL EMBROIDERED RUG

For years crewel embroidery work has been popular for draperies and upholstery fabrics. Now imaginative contemporary craftsmen have popularized its use as a striking and sophisticated area rug. Its large, wandering, open pattern is simply delightful. If you look closely at it, you will no doubt recognize many crewel embroidery stitches. It is sometimes hard to visualize these stitches as a rug, but with the finer, less looped stitches made with clipped yarns on a firm foundation, crewelwork makes a very satisfactory rug. Tight and flat, the stitches have the appearance and strength of a woven rug.

Design

Graph paper is often used for making designs. With crewel embroidery, however, the design is so free and flowing, it is best drawn on the background with a felt pen. On a large piece of brown wrapping paper, let your pen go where it will. Trial and error will bring forth the design you want. It is even more rewarding than you thought it could be.

When you walk through a museum, ideas may come to you. Something will catch your eye. Perhaps you have no plan for duplicating the design; perhaps you never could. But a bright new idea that will please you even more may result. Your hand takes the message from your mind and something fantastic appears. Where did this creation come from? Try it.

Materials

1. The background should be sturdy homespun woolen or upholstery linen. The edge of this rug can be finished with a 2-inch hem or a heavy handmade fringe. The Rya knot can be used here effectively.
2. Three-ply tapestry or a lightweight rug yarn will be right for "painting" the picture.
3. A tapestry needle, large enough to carry the yarn will be all that you'll need.
4. Dressmaker's weights sewed into the hem at intervals will keep the rug flat on the floor.
5. Brown paper and a felt pen.

Crewelwork Stitches

After studying the illustrations and directions for the following stitches, make notes on those you plan to use. Practice the following crewel stitches until you feel you are ready to work on your rug.

The Outline, or Stem, Stitch (Figure 53) is used for stems or outlining flowers. It is also good for holding down and finishing a turned-under edge. The stitches cover a given line. Working from left to right, place the needle in a slightly diagonal position pointing to the left. If each stitch is the same length, the embroidery resembles a continuous thread.

The Buttonhole Stitch (Figure 54) is used a great deal in stitchery. It is interchangeable with the blanket stitch, which is similar. Worked in a circle it forms a round flower, and with other stitches it provides variety. Used with either single or double thread, the buttonhole stitch is a pretty edge finisher. It is worked from left to right by placing the threaded needle in from the top and coming out at the bottom over the thread. This makes a rolled-looking edge. Move to the right, keeping the stitch the same length. Hold this stitch with your left hand and again come in at the top. Return to the bottom and over the thread. The space between the stitches is the same at the top and bottom.

The Closed Buttonhole Stitch (Figure 55) is especially attractive for the circular flower. It is made like the

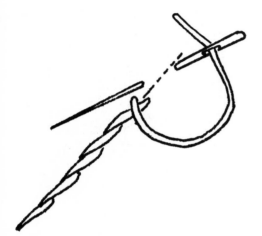

FIGURE 53 The outline, or stem, stitch.

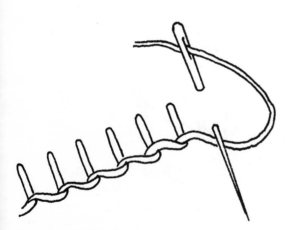

FIGURE 54 The buttonhole stitch.

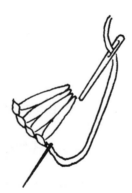

FIGURE 55 The closed buttonhole stitch.

buttonhole stitch, but very close stitches are used, and the top portion is closed.

The Feather Stitch (Figure 56) must be symmetrical, whether it is worked horizontally, diagonally, or vertically. A double or triple feather stitch can be used, but we are concerned only with the single stitch.

To make the single stitch, imagine a pattern that has two lines parallel to one another. Bring the needle from underneath to the top of the left line. Cross over to the right line and take a tiny stitch. Now the thread is looped and looks like a miniature jump rope. Come over this loop and cross to the left again. Then, as you did on the right side, take a tiny stitch under and up, making another tiny jump rope. Now go over the loop and cross to the right. Repeat this procedure until you've made all the stitches you need.

Practice feather-stitching on a piece of scrap material until your stitches are nice and even; it's a good idea to use dots as a guide until you develop a sense of spacing. Feather stitching is very decorative. But more than that, it is functional, because it can be used to anchor fabric to a foundation.

The Chain Stitch (Figure 57) is a decorative and versatile stitch which can be a filler for flowers or leaves. It can also be shaded in many colors. Singly, it forms a heavier and more interesting stem than the outline stitch. The needle starts the chain at the top. Place the needle beside the top where it came up, leaving a loop. Let the needle go through to the back and come up inside the loop and over the thread. This makes a new chain link which locks into the one before it. Continue making these links in a straight line, or turn as necessary to fill in a leaf.

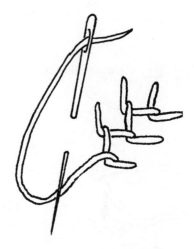

FIGURE 56 The feather stitch.

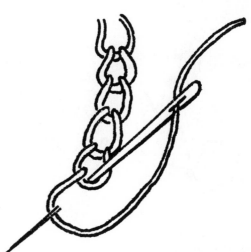

FIGURE 57 The chain stitch.

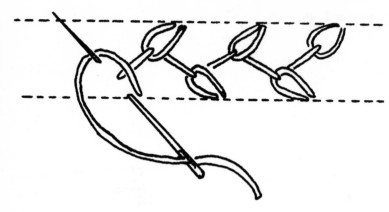

FIGURE 58 The chain feather stitch.

The Chain Feather Stitch (Figure 58) is a decorative stitch which invites many variations. It resembles a chain stitch, but swings from side to side with an elongated connecting extension in between each link.

The Zigzag Chain (Figure 59) is a chain stitch stitched to one side and then to the other. It is a versatile and unusually decorative stitch, especially when done with thread of two colors. If it is twisted, it becomes still another stitch.

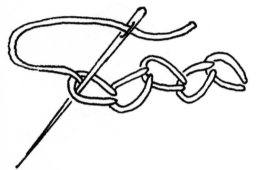

FIGURE 59 The zigzag chain.

The Lazy Daisy Stitch (Figure 60) is very much like the chain stitch. It is usually done in a circle or semicircle. It can be made in many sizes to represent petals increasing in size as the petals grow larger.

The Satin Stitch (Figure 61) might be used to make a solid edge, in which case the stitches must be close together. The stitches are parallel because the needle is put in at the same point each time. It might be worked on a scalloped edge or for the center of a flower. Used on a leaf it is most effective if it comes into the center on an angle and works toward the point. Shading also adds to the design. Some embroiderers call this the fishbone stitch.

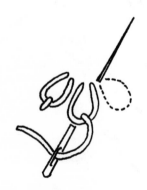

FIGURE 60 The lazy daisy stitch.

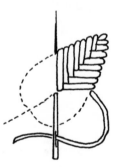

FIGURE 61 The satin stitch.

GETTING STARTED IN HANDMADE RUGS

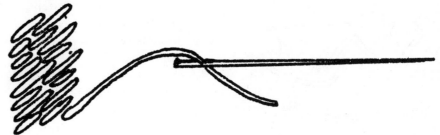

FIGURE 62 The long-and-short stitch.

The Long-and-Short Stitch (Figure 62) is great fun to do. The longer stitches can create shading from the outside of a petal. The short stitch, which varies in length, is used to fill in, making a solid and beautiful design. Very large or very small flowers can be worked this way. Branches or leaves come alive if three or four shades of green or brown are introduced.

The French Knot (Figure 63). How striking one little knot can be in the center of a solid circle flower! Tiny as the French knot is, it gives weight when placed at the end of a stamen in a flower. Serving as clusters of seeds, or used through the center of a large leaf, it adds contrast. To make the French knot, bring the needle to the surface of the material from beneath. Wrap the thread tightly around the needle several times. Do not let the thread slip. Return the needle through the cloth, close to where it came up in the beginning. Hold it as the thread follows through to the back. Move over to begin another knot, or if only one is to be made, lock the stitch.

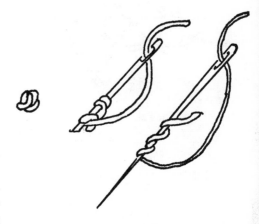

FIGURE 63 The French knot.

The Split Stitch (Figure 64) serves the same purpose as the outline stitch; however, it is less bulky. Working from left to right, anchor the thread on the underside with a knot. Take a stitch as for the outline but run the needle through the thread, separating it. Split in this way, the thread makes more of a pattern and is useful as a filler or as a stem-making stitch.

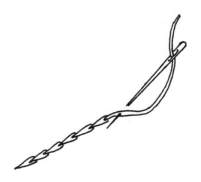

FIGURE 64 The split stitch.

BEWITCHING STITCHERY

69

FIGURE 65 The herringbone stitch.

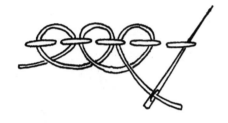

FIGURE 66 The Pekinese stitch.

The Herringbone Stitch (Figure 65) resembles a cross-stitch, but it is more decorative. It is useful for holding one piece of material against another or even for creating a pattern on an appliquéd square.

Working from left to right, place the needle on the lower line, coming from the underside. Move to the upper line on the diagonal. Go under, taking a small stitch to the left. Return to the lower line, taking a small stitch. Notice that these small stitches are all from right to left and the stitch on top is a diagonal which crosses the previous one as it travels to the top or to the bottom. You may recall seeing blanket binding put on with the herringbone stitch. In that case, the stitches on the underside hold the material securely.

The Pekinese Stitch (Figure 66) makes an attractive finishing stitch. First make a simple row of backstitches and then weave the thread through these stitches, starting at the left. Go through the second backstitch and then loop back into the first backstitch. Go into stitch 3 and loop back into backstitch 2. In other words, for every stitch ahead, drop back one. When completed, draw it up carefully. The result is a dainty little scalloped finish on top and bottom edges.

Application of Crewelwork Stitches

1. **Stems** Slender, graceful stem lines can be developed beautifully with the outline or the chain stitch (three stitches to the inch). If a stem needs more than a single line or more weight, do not use heavier yarn. Instead, use several rows, shading greens into browns, for example. (Refer also to the colcha stitch, page 72. It is quite effective for stems, leaves, and flowers.)

2. **Leaves** Leaves are every bit as important as the flowers. They can be worked in a solid chain stitch and shaded (Figure 57). The satin stitch is also effective for leaves: it adds richness, especially when slanted upward toward the tip or toward the outside edges from the center, giving the impression of leaf veins (Figure 61). Shading with the satin stitch also gives weight and a lifelike quality to the leaves.

3. **Flowers** Flowers contribute to the overall mood that dominates any design. They can be worked in the chain, colcha, or satin stitch. Try the fringed style, combining the lazy daisy

and the satin stitch with French knots in the center. French knots work up quickly and are an attractive addition to the center of any flower. They can introduce a touch of bold color which is very effective.

To make the three-dimensional fringe-style flower (Figure 67), wind the yarn around a cardboard. The size of the cardboard will determine the dimensions of the flower. If you want a large, showy flower, the cardboard should be cut and wrapped to make 3-, 4-, or 5-inch pieces of yarn. After the yarn is wrapped on the cardboard, cut along one side. These pieces of yarn will be used to make the fringe for the flower's edge.

The center is worked in a satin stitch. Surrounded by lazy daisy petals, it is finished at the tips with French knots. The fringe on the flowers is done last. There may be three rows or more, depending on how large the flower is. It may be a full or only a half circle, which is equally effective. Always begin with row number 1, or the outside area. The others will overlap as they are sewed on.

To make the fringe, take a tiny stitch with the needle pointing toward you, leaving about half of the tail of yarn leading back toward the center. Move the needle to the right one-sixth of an inch, and take another tiny stitch opposite the

FIGURE 67 Fringe flower.

first one. This time the needle points toward the center. Leave a loop hanging in the space between the stitches. Remove the needle and pull the two tails of yarn through the loop toward you, making a knot. This forms the first fringe stitch. Repeat, making stitches until the outside edge is finished. Trim the fringe to make it even. The second and successive rows will be done in the same manner.

No matter how many rows there are, the one nearest the center is always done last. Brush the finished flower and trim the edges. Shading in the rows helps to make the flower more conspicuous and effective.

The illustrations will give you ideas for your stitches. It is exciting to combine all these stitches in different ways. Make your stitches do what you want them to do.

THE COLCHA-STITCH RUG

The colcha stitch can be used in a rug or a hanging. It is one of many beautiful examples of a craft of Mexican colonial days (Plate 15). Like so much of our handwork, this decorative stitch was first used in a blanket. Later it became a decoration for a bed in the form of a spread, from which it gets its name. Colorful and closely stitched with a soft yarn on heavy material, the colcha-stitched rug brings a bit of artistry into the home.

Design

Though this embroidery is old and leans toward the traditional, it is contemporary. It is open, free, expressive, and as gratifying to the worker as oils are to the painter. Your design might be Mexican, Spanish, or Mediterranean. The colcha stitch can be supplemented by some of the finer crewelwork stitches. When making the colcha stitch, however, keep in mind the shapes of leaves, flowers, and stems; they should be worked in the same way that they grow. Follow the pattern of the veins — not crosswise, but slanting toward the tip. Stems are filled in, running with the moving line of the stem, not crosswise.

Materials

1. A list of yarn colors from a yarn chart will help you decide what to buy. These can be three- or four-ply yarns which can be separated when finer threads are needed.
2. The size of the crewel needle used will depend on the weight of the yarn.

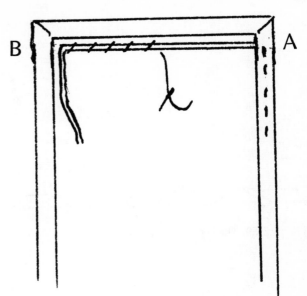

FIGURE 68 Starting the colcha rug or hanging.

3. Through the centuries the foundation was often whatever was at hand. Today you can select the material that is most suitable for your work. For a hanging that is to be very decorative, satin or velvet fabric with gold fringe, or gold and silver threads, will be right. For a rug, a heavy woolen background, heavy upholstery yardage, or a heavy woolen blanket will certainly be an excellent base.

Procedure

1. Hem the piece of material you plan to use.
2. Run the basic yarn or thread through part of the hem at A (Figure 68) to anchor and hide it without using a knot.
3. Place and pin the thread along the edge from A to B.
4. Bring the needle from beneath to make tiny holding stitches that secure the thread but are not part of the design (Figure 69).
5. Going from left to right and using a rhythm similar to doing an overcast stitch, bring the needle through on the side nearest you (Figure 69). Run a tiny diagonal stitch over the long strand; go through to the underside. Take a diagonal stitch while underneath; return to the top on the side nearest you again. Continue to do this zigzag and you will have tiny diagonal stitches holding your thread.
6. Return to B (Figure 68), pinning another long thread into position. Repeat the stitch, working from B to A. Stagger

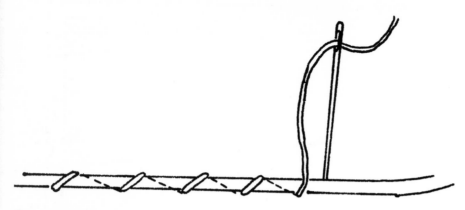

FIGURE 69 The colcha stitch.

the stitches in this row, so that they do not line up with the first ones.

You have now learned how to do the background. The stitches in the design will be made the same way. The yarn will curve and point in different directions and odd-shaped areas will have to be filled in. Keep in mind the direction of the leaves, flowers, and other patterns given earlier.

8
CARE, CLEANING, AND REPAIR OF RUGS

PROTECTING RUGS

No matter what kind of rug you have made, it deserves protection before it is placed on the floor and used. To do this, use Scotchgard or Sta-Clean, silicone products which will prevent grease and dirt from penetrating the material. Spills cannot soak in to make ugly spots, but will wipe off easily from the rug's surface. Spray the surface several times, drying between coats. This is better than one heavy saturation all at once.

It is always advisable to have your rugs protected against moths. A woven wool rug must be mothproofed, expecially if it is under a bed. Commercial treatment of rugs against moths usually carries a five-year guarantee; but if you are ambitious, you can do the job yourself. The marvelous sprays available today, which keep rugs free from pests, enable you to do a thorough job. Spray both sides of the rug every thirty days to make sure that all larvae are killed. A small glass sprayer from the dime store will do the job.

CLEANING RUGS

All types of floor coverings must be kept clean. Nothing is better than a vacuum cleaner for removing deeply embedded grit. If you do not have a suction- or agitator-type cleaner, use a broom. Lint must not be allowed to accumulate because it is a natural nest for moths.

Cleaning Braided Rugs

Braided rugs which are firm and properly laced will resist catching and holding gravel, the greatest threat to any rug. Folds kept on the left side during braiding are placed to the inside when laced against the touching braid. This means the outside braid has no open edge to the surface.

Since braided rugs are reversible, turn them over often for cleaning and longer wear.

When the first snow falls, take your rugs outside. Remove any grease spots with a cleaner. Follow this with a fine snow bath. As the snow is swept off, it will carry dust, dirt, lint, and grit with it. Clean both sides of the rug. It will not become wet enough to cause any drying problems. If you have never cleaned a rug with snow, the procedure may not sound feasible. Try it — it works. You'll do it again.

If this is not enough, or if there is no snow, remove grease spots and shampoo with any good commercial product. If you can work on a cement driveway or sidewalk, take an old-fashioned scrub brush and your shampoo, and give your braided, hooked, Indian, and Oriental rugs a good cleaning. Run the hose freely, washing the rugs clean of any loose dirt. Dry the rugs as quickly as possible by hanging each on a thick pole that is longer than the width of the rug. Hang them in the garage, between trees, or in the basement, depending on the time of year. Clotheslines are not satisfactory for rug drying, as they do not give sufficient support.

Cleaning Hooked Rugs

Some people can use hooked rugs for years and years. Other hooked rugs die an early death at careless hands.

Perfectly made hooked rugs which have a tight, close surface will last longer than loose, large-looped hooked rugs because they tend to resist soil. Conversely, the higher and coarser the pile of the hooked rug, the more difficult it will be to maintain and prolong its life. Do all you can to prevent the cutting, grinding damage of gravel to your rugs. Your efforts will be rewarded by a longer-lasting rug.

Large or small, the hooked rug cleans easily, but it should not be washed by machine. Clean it often by the shampoo method given for braided rugs. When rinsing it with the hose, use the pressure on the back of the rug to force the dirt out through the top surface. Turn it often on the pole, squeezing accumulated water from the ends and corners. Be sure it is thoroughly dry before putting it back on the floor.

Cleaning Woven Rugs

The woven rug requires little care. It may be cleaned with a vacuum cleaner or swept with a broom. This rug can be sent to the cleaners or shampooed at home in the way described for the hooked or braided rug.

REPAIRING AND RESTORING RUGS

Replacing Damaged or Cut Sections

If a corner piece or a section has been cut from your rug for a cold-air duct or a fireplace hearth, it is relatively easy to replace. Turn the rug, putting the right side against the floor, and lay the piece back into position. With overcasting stitches, sew the rug and piece together (Figure 70). Work from one edge to the corner and then from the other edge to the corner. Do not draw the stitches, but don't let them become slack either. When you are satisfied that the piece is firmly in place, put on sections of iron-on tape. Begin on an edge and run the tape to the corner, pressing with a hot iron to secure it. Follow the same procedure for the other edge, but put this second piece at a right angle to the first one.

Turn your rug over and tease the pile over the seam with a needle. After it is walked on for a short time, the pile will begin to flatten and evidence of the restoration will disappear.

In case your rug has been burned by a cigarette or damaged by moths, there are several methods for repairing it. There is always the commercial expert to turn to, but if you want to do it yourself clean out any charred particles first. Remove tufts from another rug or from a scrap, and make a base of household cement sufficient to secure them. Carpeting and rugs have been

FIGURE 70 Replacing a section of rug.

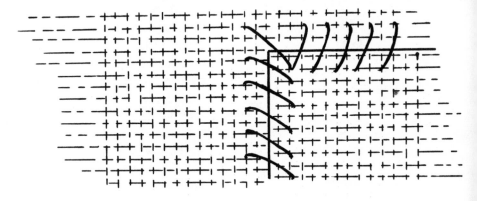

kept going for years with just this simple method. Moth holes may also be taken care of in this manner.

If a large area is damaged, clean the surface and remove any loose threads or stitches from the rug's backing until the foundation is bare. Thread your needle with tapestry yarn of the same color as the rug and take it down from the top through to the back. Come up to the top through another hole and continue this procedure until the space is filled. When you have finished, clip the yarns on top to make a new pile. Be sure this measures up to the original pile of the rug.

Repairing Woven Rugs

If a part of a woven rug should become worn, it can be replaced by reweaving a new strip into the rug with a sack needle. Color will not be important in a hit-or-miss rug, unless it is on the seam. Then it will be best to carry a shade through to join the one in the next strip, especially if the rug is large.

Repairing Hooked Rugs

There are two principal methods by which a hooked rug can be repaired. The first is by replacement after the worn area has been removed. Take away any loose loops, making room for new stitches. Starting with a hook and woolen strip or yarn, replace the missing stitches. This should be done in colors that match, even if you have to "fade" some of your material.

If you find that the burlap as well as the stitches is worn, it will be necessary to replace a part of the foundation. Sew a piece of burlap firmly on the underside. It should extend beyond the spot where the new hooking is to be done to make the repair more secure. Hook with your matching woolen strips until the area is covered. When this is done, whether on the background or the design, the rug will look like new.

Very often a hooked rug will not be damaged in the center. It is the edges that usually break first. There are several ways to repair these; the most common way is to remove the worn part. If only the stitches have worn, new ones may replace the old. However, if damage to the edges is extensive and if the ends catch in the vacuum cleaner, repair is more difficult. Use a new piece of burlap extended far enough beyond the edge so that it can be used for facing when the new hooking is finished; and before you begin to hook, be sure that the new piece is well anchored to the rug. This may be done by handsewing with stitches that are tight, but not tight enough to pucker the material.

The second repair method uses a braid. Sew a piece of burlap 6 inches wide around the rug's edge. It is best to cut the burlap to the shape of the rug but it can also be a bias piece. Sew 3 inches of the burlap piece underneath the rug's edges, leaving a 3-inch surplus to extend beyond the edge of the rug.

The outside inch of this piece should be turned over to make the top hem, which faces up on the *right side*. Make a closed braid (see Chapter 6), lay it on top of the burlap extension, and sew it to the edge of the hooked rug. Also sew through from the underside to hold it more firmly. Now lace the second closed braid onto the first braid that you have just added.

When this is done, your rug has a new substantial and long-wearing edge. If you wish to enlarge the rug, do not increase the size of the burlap. Instead, lace on additional braids.

BINDING RUGS

The ability to bind a rug or a piece of carpeting is a real money-saver. It often means salvaging something which would otherwise be discarded.

1. Measure the area that is to be bound. Carpet binding may be purchased by the yard or by the roll in department and carpet stores. This binding has a range of colors, so finding a matching or complementary color shouldn't be difficult.

2. Straighten the edges of your rug. If there are worn portions, trim them off evenly.

3. Place the right side of your rug binding against the right side of the rug. Keep the edges together.

4. Thread a heavy darning needle with carpet thread to match the binding.

5. Sew from right to left through the back of the rug into the tape (Figure 71). Take a ½-inch diagonal stitch into the third wire of the back of the rug. ("Wire" is the word used for "ridge" by commercial rugmakers.) The stitch returns,

FIGURE 71 Sewing binding tape to the front of the rug.

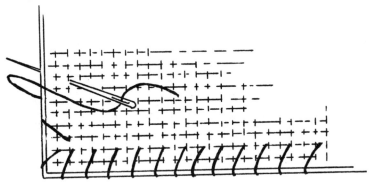

CARE, CLEANING, AND REPAIR OF RUGS

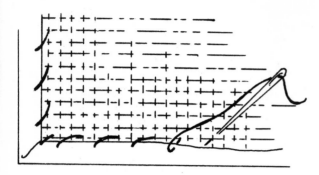

FIGURE 72 Sewing binding tape to the back of the rug.

buried in the pile. The needle comes out through the tape, very close — 1/8 inch — to the edge. The stitches are ½ inch long on the wrong side but short on the right side, thus preventing them from showing. Continue sewing until the edge is done.

6. When you reach a corner, do not pull the tape. Ease it around the area. Later it may be mitered.

7. When the edges of the rug have been bound, turn the tape over and against the back of the rug. Only a small part of the tape should show from the right side. Do not draw it so tight that the stitches show.

8. Sewing from left to right, attach the tape to the back of the rug with stitches 1 inch apart (Figure 72). Hold the rug with the wrong side to you. The tape's unsewed edge will be facing you. Put the point of your needle through the tape first. Then pick up the wires. The needle points toward you. Come through the tape 1/4 inch from the selvage. Pick up only a double wire when making these stitches. If you bend the rug slightly, it will be easier to pick up the wires.

9. If you are binding only a straight edge, the ends will need to be folded in and overcast. However, where there are corners to contend with, it will be necessary to miter them. Sometimes this can be done by folding in surplus material before sewing the last edge down against the back of the rug. If there seems to be too much thickness, trim some of the material.

If you have an old carpet with worn sections, remove the good parts and bind the edges, making several rugs from it. Pieces of new and used carpet or remnants, when bound on all four edges, make fine stair treads. These are like small rugs, and if tacked down, give long service. Make a few extra treads and you will be surprised at the additional wear they will give.

Don't be afraid to put fringe on a rug as a finish. Today's commercial fringes have a double edge and the rug fits in between, thus saving labor and also eliminating the skill formerly needed to do the job. This edge now forms three thicknesses — the rug and the two edges of the fringe. It may be sewed on a power machine, but a thimble, linen thread, and a strong needle will help you to sew this on very satisfactorily by hand, if it is necessary. Examine commercially fringed rugs in stores and you will realize how simple they are to apply.

Binding Oriental Rugs

Nothing is more beautiful than an Oriental rug. On the other hand, nothing is more unsightly than a rug whose edges are worn and frayed. You can re-edge your rug by using tapestry yarn and a buttonhole stitch, but it will wear better if you use the old rugmaker's method — going over and over the edge with a binding stitch, satin-stitch style. Put the threaded needle in from the top of the rug. Work from right to left. Be sure to keep the edge even where the needle goes into the rug.

For worn areas in the designs of these and other rugs, watercolors or crayolas can help to hide the defects.

BIBLIOGRAPHY

BOOKS

Anders, Nedda C., *Applique Old and New*. New York, Hearthside Press, Inc., 1967.

Atwater, Mary Meigs, *Byways in Handweaving*. New York, The Macmillan Co., 1954.

———, *The Shuttle-Craft Book of American Hand-Weaving*. New York, The Macmillan Co., 1951.

Bates, Kenneth, *Basic Design*. Cleveland, Ohio, World Publishing Co., 1960.

Beitler, Ethel J., *Create with Yarn*. Scranton, Pa., International Textbook Co., 1964.

Black, Mary E., *New Key to Weaving*. Bruce Publishing Co., 1961.

Blumenau, Lili, *The Art and Craft of Handweaving*. New York, Crown Publishers, 1955.

Brinley, Rosemary, *Plaiting*. New York, Dover Publications, Inc., 1952.

Butler, Anne, *Embroidery Stitches*. New York, Frederick A. Praeger, Inc., 1968.

James, Rebecca, *Colcha Stitch*. Santa Fe, N.M., International Museum of Folk Art, 1963.

Karasz, Mariska, *Adventures in Stitches and More Adventures, Fewer Stitches*. New York, Funk & Wagnalls Co., 1959.

Krevitsky, Nik, *Stitchery: Art and Craft*. New York, Van Nostrand Reinhold Co., 1966.

Lawless, Dorothy, *Rug Hooking and Braiding*, rev. ed. New York, Thomas Y. Crowell Co., 1962.

Mathews, Sibyl I., *Needle-Made Rugs*. New York, Hearthside Press, Inc., 1960.

Rainey, Sarita R., *Weaving Without a Loom*. Worcester, Mass., Davis Publications, Inc., 1966.

Sydney, Sylvia, *Needlepoint Book*. New York, Van Nostrand Reinhold Co., 1968.

Thorpe, Heather G., *A Handweaver's Workbook*. New York, The Macmillan Co., reissue 1966.

Tod, Osma G., *The Joy of Hand-Weaving*, 2d ed. New York, Van Nostrand Reinhold Co., 1964.

Wilson, Erica, *Crewel Embroidery*. New York, Charles Scribner's Sons, 1962.

Wilson, Jean, *Weaving Is for Anyone*. New York, Van Nostrand Reinhold Co., 1966.

Znamierowski, Nell, *Step-by-Step Weaving*. New York, Golden Press, Inc., 1967.

PERIODICALS AND PAMPHLETS

Craft Horizons, Vol. XXIV, No. 3. Special issue, *The American Craftsman* (May-June 1964).

Fabric for Living, a text researched and prepared by Mrs. Frances Kilham and Mrs. Marjorie F. Lambert for a special exhibition held at the Museum of International Folk Art, Santa Fe, N.M., March 27, 1967 through January 7, 1968.

Good Housekeeping, "Needle Craft" (1970-1971).

———, "Handweaver and Craftsman" (Winter 1970).

INDEX